Regeneration and Belonging

Cycle C Sermons for the First Half of the
Season After Pentecost
Based on the Gospel Lessons

I0136501

Julianna Wehrfritz-Hanson

CSS Publishing Company, Inc.
Lima, Ohio

REGENERATION AND BELONGING

FIRST EDITION
Copyright © 2024
by CSS Publishing Co., Inc.

Library of Congress Cataloging-in-Publication Data

Names: Wehrfritz-Hanson, Julianna, author.
Title: Regeneration and belonging / by Julianna Wehrfritz-Hanson.
Description: Lima, OH : CSS Publishing Company, Inc., 2024. | Includes
    bibliographical references.
Identifiers: LCCN 2024033631 | ISBN 9780788031250 (paperback)
Subjects: LCSH: Revelation--Christianity. | Jesus Christ--Divinity. |
    Trinity.
Classification: LCC BT127.3 .W43 2024 | DDC 231.7/4--dc23/eng/20240904
LC record available at https://lccn.loc.gov/2024033631

For more information about CSS Publishing Company resources, visit our website at www.csspub.com, email us at csr@csspub.com, or call (800) 241-4056.

e-book:
ISBN-13: 978-0-7880-3126-7
ISBN-10: 0-7880-3126-0

ISBN-13: 978-0-7880-3125-0
ISBN-10: 0-7880-3125-2

PRINTED IN USA

Dedicated to Garth, my husband and colleague of many years who has shared the challenges and blessings of preaching and of living the word for all the years of our marriage.

Contents

Preface

This book of thirteen sermons for the season of Pentecost, series C in the church year is intended to be a resource for those who preach or are interested in preaching.

In the life of a busy preacher, it can be helpful to read the sermons of other preachers to see how they worked through and presented themes, or a flow of thought in a text. Along the way the reader may discover a new approach or insight which may be incorporated into their own work.

It is my hope and expectation that these sermons will be of assistance to those preparing to write their own sermons, and provide inspiration. Some of the illustrations, or analogies may be of use as well.

These sermons are also available to lay preachers who lead public worship services, and may struggle with the task of writing a sermon. This resource may be of assistance in that effort to prepare for preaching.

When attending seminary one of the professors who was teaching a course of preaching encouraged the students to continue reading the sermons of others in the future. This practice is a means to encounter other ways of approaching familiar texts in the scriptures and applying them to the challenges the listeners face.

As one encounters the words and connections made by other preachers at times it may also open one to other perspectives and ways of approaching the task of preaching. A further benefit can be the challenge to one's thinking and understanding of the texts or subjects to be engaged in the proclaimed word. Along with this, it may provide a new approach to a familiar text, and encourage some further reflection about it.

If this collection of sermons can provide these benefits, then the intention of this preacher and writer will have been accomplished. This collection of sermons is commended to those reading them to use in their own work" of preaching. May they be an aid to those who sit before an empty page looking for inspiration and material to present for those who will be hearing and receiving what they will be proclaiming through the preached word. May the glory and good purposes of God be served through the word and the preaching of it.

Trinity Sunday
John 16:12-15

Truth?

What is truth? This basic question was asked by Pontius Pilate of Jesus as he stood there before the Roman governor.

These days a variety of answers may be given to this query. There is the scientific answer that would define the truth as that which is verifiable through the evidence of the senses and supported by repeated experimentation or observation performed by independent laboratories producing the same results. Others might say that truth is defined by an individual in regard to their own experiences.

Others would deem truth as something defined by the state, where what is deemed true is seen as malleable, and history as adjustable to the ideology of the political system, and its propaganda.

In response to Pontius Pilate's question, Jesus' approach to this issue was that he came to testify to the truth and that everyone who belongs to him hears his voice. Jesus was the bearer of truth, and if we would learn that truth, particularly with things ultimate, then it is necessary that we attend to the voice of Christ. As such, the kind of truth that Jesus shared was tied up with the relationship with himself and the other two members of the Trinity. According to Jesus, truth was not merely contained in the facts or empirical definitions. Something more was needed than what was primarily used in this world to discern what is true about the realities of life, the substance of this world, and the universe. Yet a different understanding of truth is needed when dealing with a God and creator who is in the midst of the world and yet hidden from us in our mortal condition. How shall we really know this God who creates and who knows the entire truth if we cannot encounter this One through our senses of sight, hearing, touch, or taste? How do we test the truth of this maker and redeemer that does not fit under the lens of a microscope nor seen through a telescope? To encounter the truth coming from God or information about who the divine is, requires quite a different approach than the one we usually employ to discern the truth from that which is imaginary or the untrue.

Before the coming of Jesus, God was revealed through the words of the prophets and the kinds of experiences that fulfilled the words of these messengers of the divine. In Jesus, God was revealed in who Christ is, what he taught and did for us and the sake of the world. Jesus was the clearest revelation of the truth about who God is and the will of the divine.

Jesus answered Pontius Pilate about what truth is, with the statement that, he "came into the world to testify to the truth and those who belong to the truth listen to his voice." Access to that kind of truth comes through "belonging" to the truth. The truth is gained through belonging and relationship with the one who holds and knows what is really real. So how do we come to belong to the truth?

In the text before us this day, another part of this puzzle is made known. Verse thirteen teaches this about the truth and how we are able to access it. When the Spirit of truth comes it will guide you into all the truth, and this one speaks not on its own from self but shares what has been heard. This text helps us to understand the place and importance of the Holy Spirit who is also called the spirit of truth. We are not left to figure out this most important truth by ourselves but are guided and enabled to comprehend it through the working of the Spirit of truth. Yet there are limits on our capacity to understand, and in what is revealed.

Jesus tells his disciples that he has much to tell them but recognizes that they cannot bear it at that present moment. While these ones are willing to listen to Jesus they cannot bear or carry all that he could tell them.

The question arises from Jesus' comment to the disciples about what kinds of things make them or us unable to bear the further truth that Jesus would share with us? There may have been several factors that handicapped their capacity to really hear and to be able to bear the additional truth he could have told them.

One factor may have been that they simply could not comprehend what he would have said. Sometimes in life one needs to have the knowledge or the lived experience to really understand what is being said to us. Just imagine if the disciples had been told about DNA or about computer programs and games at that time in history. Such information certainly would have gone right over their heads. It would have seemed like someone's overactive imagination at work! In this present age, there is much that we do not comprehend with the wide variety and depth of knowledge that has been gained over the past century.

A while ago, someone was talking about his grown children and when trying to talk about the work of the son, the father said that he didn't quite know what to say about the son's work. He was a physicist working in a university doing research and teaching. Yet the details of what he was working on went beyond the normal frame of reference. If one doesn't have the expertise in that area, it is difficult to grasp what that person is talking about. It can be a challenge to even understand the terminology used about a given subject. Probably the disciples were not yet sufficiently trained or developed in understanding to grasp the more advanced kinds of truth that Jesus could have shared. This would imply that there is need for growth in faith and experience with the divine in order to be able to receive and comprehend that additional truth which is yet to be revealed. Some things are only revealed as one matures in faith and grows deeper in the capacity to love and understand. As an acquaintance liked to say, "More will be revealed."

At this point in the gospel, the disciples have not yet witnessed or experienced the death of Jesus on the cross, and what would follow with his resurrection. He did try to prepare them and told them what was coming. But it likely seemed incomprehensible to them before the crucifixion happened. After Christ's passion, they would be in a state to better grasp what he had shared with them prior to his death. Then there was the work afterwards of understanding the impacts of his passion on them and their relationship with Jesus. Only after his death would they begin to understand a larger truth about who Jesus is and what he can accomplish for us now and in the future. There were important truths that they since could not grasp until after his resurrection and the time he spent with them following the resurrection.

Another factor that may have interfered with the disciples' capacity to fully bear the truth of Jesus was that they were not emotionally able to bear that further word. There are times in life when, because of the state we are in, things get past us. Times when we are emotionally distraught, or depressed, or confused, these may be times when we feel that we could not bear another thing. At such times, we may draw into ourselves just to be able to manage or to get through what is happening in our lives. Sometimes we are so absorbed in trying to resolve an issue or sort out a conflict that we may not receive other kinds of information. When we are caught up in something and focused upon it, other communications directed at us may pass us by.

There are other times when we feel too weak or unable to bear anymore. It may seem enough to get through the days and nights. When we are in a state of deep grief or are seriously ill, when we struggle to get through the basics of our lives, then we seek stability and support. It usually a time of just trying to hold steady and go with what is familiar. Those are times when we again turn to the truth that Jesus cares for us, is present with us and will help us into the future. That may be enough for that point in time.

As we consider this text, we are challenged to reflect upon what is preventing us from being able to more fully bear that further truth that Jesus would share with us. What stands in our way so that we are unable to move forward into those truths that Jesus waits to share with us? If the Spirit of truth seeks to disclose the full truth to us, then it makes sense that we can turn to that Spirit to reveal to us the truth about what impedes us from being able to bear that more complete message that Jesus would proclaim to us.

This text reminds us that Jesus knows when we cannot bear more of the word of truth and he waits for us. Jesus helps us through challenging times too, when we hopefully will be more open to receiving the truth that he would reveal to us. Perhaps it is in the tough times that we grow and our perspective is enlarged, or we learn important truths that we had not yet grasped. Jesus is patient with us and works with the Holy Spirit to get through to us enabling us to become more receptive to the added truth that he would share with us.

In the John 16:12 text, Jesus did not share further information with the disciples recognizing that they couldn't bear anymore. However, that did not mean that this added truth would be lost. Rather it may require an avenue to carry it to them when the time is right.

Even though the disciples were not able to bear the many things that Jesus could have shared he told them that when the spirit of truth came, it would continue the work of communicating that truth. Furthermore, the Spirit would not work from a lone ranger stance but will relay what has been heard. The Spirit is a conduit for the ongoing work of divine truth and revelation.

During the pandemic, a small rural congregation faced some unexpected challenges in terms of worship services. The pastor was providing a service online through the internet. However, this didn't work for the elderly in the church who didn't have a computer, nor did they know how to use it. Secondly, because the internet service was tenuous at times it did not always perform when needed. So, the pastor wound up supplying a service online, as well as by phone.

This was a reminder of how important avenues of communication are to us. Jesus had very important truth to share with those who belong to the truth and like the rural pastor strongly desires to get the message to his followers even today. If the Holy Spirit had not been active on conveying the truth proclaimed by Christ it is very likely that the message would have been lost over the years.

Instead, the Spirit of truth picked up the ball of Jesus' ministry and teaching and carried it forward. Recently I caught a clip of an exciting football game on the "news". It showed a player charging down the field with the ball and just as he was tackled by a couple of players from the opposing team, he was able to lob the ball to another player on his team who was not far from the goal. That player caught the ball and got it through the goal posts to a victory. The work of catching and passing the ball was based on good teamwork and sharing among those who are part of the group in order to win the game. That same dynamic of teamwork within the Trinity is exposed in the text from John 16:12-15.

Jesus has come and brought the truth that he bears with the heavenly parent. After Jesus' death and resurrection, the Spirit takes what is of Jesus and continues to carry it forward. That Spirit comes to reveal all truth. So, while the disciples were not able to bear all that Jesus could have shared with them, the Spirit of truth will continue the work of revealing that truth as the disciples are ready to receive it.

The Spirit doesn't have a new truth, rather receives the "ball" of truth as served to it through Christ and carries it to the others who become part of the team of those who belong to the truth. As the text says, the Spirit will take what belongs to Jesus and declare it to the disciples and us.

This text was shared with the disciples who also were commissioned to carry out the word of Christ. In so doing they joined in the work of the Holy Spirit in the transmission of the truth of God's word born into the world and our lives. In a way, this work of bearing and speaking the truth that Christ came to embody and proclaim is to join in the work of the Trinity. This message is so vital that God seeks to have it announced and shared with all who belong to the truth. This wonderful news sets us free. Even as the message about Jesus' life, death, and resurrection came to set us free from the way of sin, bondage, darkness, and death. As we join in this life-giving work, we are drawn into the mission and the way of our triune God and the truth that abides therein.

An important part of the work of this Spirit of truth is faithfulness and fidelity to what Jesus proclaimed and did for us.

I remember when I was younger, hearing my father being concerned about "high fidelity" in the quality of audio equipment he bought at that time. He explained that the higher the "fidelity" the closer it was to the original sounds. That certainly was preferable to the distortions that are associated with a poorer quality product. When we listen to older movies or recordings from the past, we certainly can notice the difference and distortion in sound compared to the quality of recording in this age.

Fidelity is important to the transmission of the truth of Christ as well. The Spirit who is so necessary in spreading the word of God, can be trusted to keep the message true and faithful to the Christ and his word. It is important that this significant word of Christ not be distorted or garbled or so distorted that it can't be understood. It is vital that the truth of the word must be preserved with fidelity.

Where the Spirit of truth moves beyond what Jesus taught and the message of his passion is that the Spirit also will reveal what is to come. Although Jesus did speak of the future, there is much that is not shared. Maybe that is part of what Jesus felt the disciples cannot bear.

Yet in this sharing of the truth of Christ, the Spirit also glorifies him. Perhaps a part of that glorification is that the Spirit lifts up the message and the person of Jesus. Dr. William Hordern wrote a book a number of years ago called, *The Holy Spirit, The Shy Member of the Trinity*. As the title indicated, his insight was that the Spirit was not about calling glory to self but rather pointing to the other members of the Trinity and supporting their work and word. The Spirit of truth is certainly a team player and a reliable support to the ongoing work of the Triune God.

We can understand the importance of giving glory, or at least recognition where it is due. I receive a magazine as an alumnus of the University of Alberta. It shares articles about some of the research being done at the university. There are also articles about people who have or are making contributions to their areas of expertise or the institution as a whole. As researchers share what they are doing and some of their findings, it is always good to see them acknowledge the work and support of others who have gone before them. It is an expression of acknowledgment that these later researchers or teachers are building on the prior insight or support of those who have gone before them. As well, it is good to see the work and contribution of students and associates recognized for their part in the projects being done.

We see this same kind of dynamic at work in the activities of the Spirit of truth. It takes what belongs to Christ and declares it to us faithfully and gives glory to him and in the process also preserves what has been shared between the Christ and the heavenly parent. For Jesus says in this text that "all that the Father has is mine, for this reason I said that (the Spirit) will take what is mine and declare it to you." In this text, one hears about the sharing of the truth between the members of the Trinity and the support among them in their effort to convey the truth of God. The interconnectedness, the mutual support and effort to proclaim the truth is vital to the work of the Trinity for us and the world.

We who belong to the truth through the work of grace and the Spirit of truth seek to listen well for that word from our Triune God and to join in the work of sharing and spreading the truth revealed most clearly in Jesus Christ. May the Spirit and word be at work enabling us to ever more fully hear that word, to live in it, and carry it forward so that others who belong to the truth may also hear, and follow the Word who speaks to us as well.

Amen.

Released

The younger man lived in an old hotel on the edge of downtown. Since he had been and could be violent as well as unpredictable and erratic, he had no friends. His family had withdrawn from him. Medications were prescribed for him, but mostly he didn't take them.

Once a week a social worker would stop by with some groceries. But she didn't feel safe around him either. She would open the door, push the boxes of groceries that she brought into the room and leave.

There continues to be people who suffer like the Gerasene demoniac. They live in our communities, even though they likely do not live in the graveyards. They live on the fringes in so many ways. How are we impacted when we have such an unpredictable and maybe violent person in our family or in our neighborhood? There are those who struggle with mental health issues but are not violent, yet needing care and support. How do we support those who are being affected by severe mental health issues, or anger issues and violence and how do care for their families?

I remember an elderly woman I met many years ago who lived in distress. She loved her son, but he was violent and easily angered. He had damaged her, and her property, and she was afraid of him. Although she turned to social services for some aid, no one seemed to be able to protect her. Consequently, she lived afraid and on edge. He had been in an institution, but the government changed its policy on what to do with those who were institutionalized with mental health issues. The government had closed most of its psychiatric facilities and released those who had lived there, back onto the streets and into their communities. So, this son terrorized his mother and others around him.

What is needed by society and by us in order to address these kinds of important matters in our midst? It's not easy. These issues continue to arise and call for some better ways of working with them. Although there are medications that may be of some assistance for some people.

What about those who do not regularly take their medications or cannot access them for lack of funds?

Often those who struggle with severe mental health challenges feel exiled or removed from the community and may be alienated from family. Just as the man living amid the tombs on that far shore of the Lake of Galilee must have felt outside of human society. What a desolate feeling that must have been, and is, for those who find themselves alone and cut off from the usual connections and interactions of social and familial life. Loneliness is another aspect of the distress associated with mental health conditions. It was likely a part of the experience of the man among the tombs. Steep loneliness is a difficult state to bear.

In Jesus' day, members of the community came with chains and bonds to bring this person dwelling among the tombs under control. But that did not work because he simply broke the chains and bindings and continued as before. It would seem that they saw no other way to handle the situation. Therefore, they tried to contain this man and reduce the threat that others felt from him. Perhaps they felt that his was a hopeless case.

This healing story happens across the Sea of Galilee opposite Capernaum where Jesus lived. The location for this healing of a man troubled with demons is important. Among scholars there is debate about the name and place where this man had belonged. However, this identification of the man being a "Gerasene" is confusing because there were a number of towns in that area with similar names.

> **Gergesa** — this town is not to be confused with either Gerasa or Gadara. Gergesa is located, with relative certainty, midway along the east bank of the Sea of Galilee; Gadara is six miles southeast from the south end of the Sea of Galilee; and Gerasa is some 35 miles southeast.
>
> The fact that Matthew places the healing of "Legion" in the "country of the Gadarenes" whereas Mark and Luke place it in the "country of the Gerasenes" may be harmonized on the historical grounds that geographical boundaries overlapped, and on the exegetical consideration that "country" embraced a wide area around the cities. Further, the conclusion seems warranted that there was confusion in some manuscripts of Gerasa with the more likely site for the miracle near Gergesa.[1]

1   https://www.biblegateway.com/resources/encyclopedia-of-the-bible/Gerasa-Gerasenes

If one has actually visited this area, it certainly fits with the details of the biblical account. On that side of the sea of Galilee a steep cliff rises from the shore. One can see where any animal or person falling off that steep edge and unto the shore hundreds of feet below would have been seriously injured or killed.

In spite of the fact that there were several places that had similar names they all were in what we now call Syria, or the Golan Heights. This territory was a gentile area. It is thought that the Hellenistic or Greek culture had strongly influenced that area in Syria. Ruins of temples to various Greek gods have been discovered in the that area and may have included the worship of the god Zeus. And, sacrifices of pigs may have been made to Zeus. This in turn would explain why there was such a large group of pigs in the area.

In light of the Jewish belief in monotheism, this worship of other gods was understood to make the gentiles unclean. This in turn would become a major issue in the spread of the early church beyond Israel in that the gentiles were considered polluted and that association with them would contaminate a faithful Jew. Too close association such as eating with Gentiles, was forbidden. Furthermore, another element of the corruption of the gentiles is their eating of unclean foods including pork. Certainly, the inclusion of the reference to such a group of swine nearby would be a further expression of the unclean and the offensive dynamics of this man's situation.

Spiritually this practice of worshiping other gods or spirits and the eating of unclean foods along with the lack of following the ritualistic practices around cleansing laid out in the torah would have led the Jews in the area to avoid such "contaminated" folk. Another aspect of this sense of corruption was that the dead were deemed unclean. There are various practices and instructions about cleanliness around dealing with the dead in the Jewish teachings. If the dead were seen as unclean, then the place of the dead certainly would have also been seen as dirty.

On a spiritual level, the Jews thought that all this uncleanliness would provide the conditions for the gentiles to be invaded by demons. Even at a spiritual level those who lived such a pagan life were understood to be polluted by their idolatry and profane lives.

The importance of the Jewish regulations around cleanliness had an impact even when they immigrated from Israel to live among the gentiles. During the dark ages when plagues were sweeping through communities in Europe and Russia, the Jews were following their guidelines about washing, especially after handling the dead. While their gentile neighbors would work with corpses then went to eat without washing their hands.

Because of their practices around cleanliness, the Jews did not die at the same rate as their gentile neighbors. The gentiles noticed this difference in the death rate between themselves and the Jews. At that time people did not know about bacteria, and viruses and their connection to illness even death, so they looked at other factors or "explanations" about why the Jews were not dying at the same rate as themselves.

It does make sense that they would be looking for explanations for this. Unfortunately, some of the possibilities they considered morphed into lies. One of those lies was the charge that the Jews were poisoning the wells. As a result of this lie, the other people in the communities then held the Jews responsible for the illness killing so many. The gentiles then reacted by beating and murdering the Jews, destroying their property and means of making a living and driving them from the area. These attacks on the Jews and their settlements are called "Pogroms" and they experienced many of them. This misunderstanding about the power and significance of cleansing and seeking to live a clean life led to major suffering for the Jews and added to the growth of antisemitism.

In the Jewish perspective, this is a story about an unclean gentile living an unclean life in an unclean place, close to a herd of unclean animals. It is one layer of contamination upon another. They might consider this a dirty story.

Yet, being a Jew and knowing all the teaching around cleanliness, one would think and expect Jesus as well as his disciples to avoid such a man. Jesus was not scared off by this man and his condition. Jesus was not contained or limited by the regulations that would separate him from others even those deemed unfit and contaminated. Jesus understood the great need of this fellow standing on the shore waiting for Jesus' care and mercy. Jesus comes, steps off the boat and meets the man living among the dead. One wonders if Jesus had heard about this fellow and had intentionally come across the Sea of Galilee to meet and help him. Those spirits who dwelt in the man recognize who was standing before him, and this time the voices within were afraid.

Jesus asked the name of the evil that controlled this fellow and the answer is "Legion" for there was a whole crowd of evil presences within him. These demons can recognize Jesus and know that their gig is up. Jesus *would* send them out. They knew that they could not refuse his order only negotiate the destination to which they would be sent. One option was the "abyss". It obviously was a most dreaded destination. Interestingly, Jesus obliged them and sent them into the swine nearby.

So, what did those demons do when they were given other living creatures to inhabit? They caused the pigs to run over the cliff, into the lake below, and to their death. Bodies of water were understood to be places inhabited by evil spirits so they were returning to their element.

We read of other dismissals of demons in the gospel, in this text Jesus was up against a great number of them. This legion of demons present, and their obligation to obey his word, demonstrated the extent of his power. Even together these demons can offer Jesus no opposition. His word was obeyed. His authority was full and final for the fate of this group of evil invaders.

On the cross, Jesus would take on the great force of evil, and though it sought to destroy him even in death the power of the forces opposed to God and the Christ would not destroy him. Though Jesus died, he would cast off death. Jesus promised that those who have faith in him would also be delivered from the force and oppression of evil. In the end, Christ would have the final word over all the forces of evil and death. The day would come when they would no longer enter or control human beings or the creatures of the earth.

Jesus had the capacity and the power to set this man so infested by evil free from what had so up-ended his life, with just some conversation and a command. Although it cost a herd of pigs their lives, Jesus did not just confine this troubled and agitated soul as others had tried to do. Rather, Jesus acted to release him from that which had oppressed this tormented man and taken over his life. In doing this, Jesus set this man free and restored him to sanity as well as normal life.

What the fellow on the shore needed was cleansing, that was the method of his healing and restoration. Jesus had the capacity to deliver that release from what had cluttered, contaminated, and controlled the fellow's life to the point of incapacity. Soap and water were not the means of accomplishing the release from that kind of filth, rather it is accomplished by the authority and the word of Jesus.

While most of us have plenty of water and soap to clean the outside of our bodies and our clothes, we appreciate that we can enjoy cleanliness.

There are times when we also feel befouled by the things that have happened to us or the things that we have done. Or we have gotten caught up in dynamics that have brought harm to another and then we feel badly about those actions and words. Soap and water can't scrub away the sense of inner contamination. It is difficult to carry that sense of guilt or shame or violation with us. Even as Jesus came to seek out the man so disturbed by the evil within, so Jesus came to seek us and to release us from what had befouled and darkened our lives. His power was able to release us, and we are glad even as the former demoniac was.

What a tremendous liberation that must have been for the man who had lived among the tombs. He could leave his dwelling place as the living dead among the dead. He could leave behind the intense torment, loneliness and isolation that had been his lot. That which polluted his inner being was cleansed away. The torment had come to an end, and he was free to be restored to his place in society and family. Unhindered by the influences that drove him, now this freed man could participate in the family, community, maybe take up work, its labor, contribution and benefits. One can imagine this fellow's sense of liberation.

This story lifts up the mission of Jesus who had come to set us free from the power of sin, evil, and death. He had the capacity to do this not only for the man on the shore of Lake Galilee, but he came seeking us, willing to liberate, and able to cleanse us from the evil and uncleanliness that troubles us as well.

Sometimes we too have to deal with difficult mental, emotional, or practical conditions in our lives. It may feel like life is spinning out of control and that we have lost our way in life. Like the Gerasene demoniac, we also may not know where to find the help needed or feel that we have no one to assist us. Other forces and dynamics seem to gain control over our life and future, and we can find ourselves in dark places, unable to find the path through the distress into a better life. Consequently, one lives day to day just getting by or maybe not. In the midst of difficulties, sometimes we find ourselves alone, and not know if or how we can move forward. The situation may feel like a hopeless case.

Fortunately, Jesus who was not scared off by the severe condition of the Gerasene demoniac and his alienation from friends, family, or community. Jesus arrived without chains and bonds with which to restrain this disturbed man. Rather, Jesus came with the capacity to remove that which was creating the chaos and degradation of the man on the shore. Instead of just trying to deal with the behaviors, Jesus got to the root of the disturbance in this man's life.

Likewise, Christ would not avoid us or be frightened away from us regardless of whatever seemingly unmanageable situation we find ourselves in. Nor is he deterred by the reaction and comments of others who might also want to cast us out or judge us. He will be there to meet us where we are at. Jesus came across the lake of Galilee and engaged the one labelled a "demoniac" who lived there. Jesus was greeted by this person who had come to him, able to identify who he was. Jesus did not simply get back in the boat and push off from shore with his disciples. Rather, he stayed and talked with this man who so needed care and healing even when he seemed beyond help. Jesus stayed and exercised his capacity to restore this terribly lost, and unclean person releasing him from what kept him down. In Jesus is hope for us as well, even in the face of severe challenges, and the sense of being out of control, Jesus can settle us too.

It is into these very circumstances that Jesus showed up, even if others forsake us. He had the capacity to address the root of the problem bringing relief and comfort. Through the story of the man among the tombs, we are reminded that Jesus is stronger than the power of darkness and evil. His word was sufficient to expel that which had captured and contained the man whom Jesus came to set free.

The magnitude of the large swineherd's loss reflects the greatness of Jesus' power to dismiss evil or demonic powers.

The same Jesus can come to us then through the word address the darkness including the things that would confine us or oppress us in order to set us free as well.

The name "Gerasene" means "regenerate." That certainly is a fitting name for the man who Jesus rescued from his life amid the tombs. Through the power of Christ's liberation, his life was regenerated and renewed. Now he was free to leave the tombs, return to family and society being "in his right mind", then able to function appropriately in relation to others around him. This man's life had been regenerated through the power of Jesus and his word.

At times we, like the Gerasene demoniac, get caught in the dynamics of having to deal with our own "demons" that oppress or leave us in a place a deep darkness and despair. Christ can come to those who await him on the shores of their lives, waiting for release, and regeneration. Christ has the capacity to set us free and to grant us a better life. To him we look in trust and hope.

Amen.

Welcomed Or Not

In the Shakespearean play *Romeo and Juliet* because of a dispute and alienation between their families a boundary had been created to keep the members of those families apart. They were not to associate with each other. A sense of offense certainly can lead to this kind of hostile separation which can carry on for generations.

That sort of alienation had developed between the Samaritans and the Jews over the centuries and there was social pressure to keep those of either side from relating to persons on the other side of the divide. Jesus was heading toward Jerusalem and has sent his disciples to prepare for his coming though the territory of the Samaritans. Samaria lies between the territories of Galilee in the north and Judah in the south, and on and around Mount Gerizim in the mountainous area that runs through central Israel. This mountain is 2,890 feet above sea level and has an oval shape with a flat top and steep sides flowing from the elevated plateau. For this reason, it called a "watch tower" mountain, obviously it held a good defensive position. [2]

Jesus and his disciples were crossing boundaries and are not welcome as Jews in the area inhabited by the Samaritans. Most Jews, understanding the friction between themselves and the Samaritans just avoided that route between the north and south of the country, although the road by Mount Gerizim was a main route between the north and south as well as east and west. It was a significant intersection. But Jesus didn't avoid this road but takes it intending to enter into that Samaritan territory and engage those who lived there. Yet when they do not welcome his arrival, he does not react in anger and violence as suggested by his disciples who were offended by the reaction of the Samaritans. Instead, Jesus just went by them and continues on his way. This is an expression of his outlook as a person of peace. He doesn't choose to take offense at a refusal, or lack of hospitality but continues on the path to his destination.

---

2   Paul J. Achtemeier, ed. *Harper's Bible Dictionary*, (New York and Toronto: The Society of Biblical Literature: 1985) pp.340-41

One wonders what would have happened if the inhabitants of the town where Jesus wanted to stop had been willing to welcome him. He was willing to engage them and would have brought his wisdom, his gifts and presence to them, but they did not want him in their town.

Sometimes, we also are affected by the attitudes and what is said about another group of people. Those with whom our circle says we are not to associate. There is the social pressure to comply with the keeping of those boundaries which exclude others. If one defies such regulation then the risk is that one will also be excluded, looked down upon or gossiped about for not observing the boundaries of belonging. In such circumstances, who do we miss? Whose good gifts and perspective might have blessed us, yet that is missed because of the refusal to engage the other who is deemed unacceptable for some reason?

If the Samaritan communities who refused to receive Jesus and his disciples would have welcomed him then they might have heard his insight which he shared with a Samaritan woman he met at a well as reported in John 4:4-26. There he asked water of her and engaged in conversation. Then he told her that the day was coming when true worshipers would worship not on Mount Gerizim or in Jerusalem but would worship in spirit and in truth. The implication was that the physical place of worship would not be as important as the worship in spirit and in truth. In a way, Jesus was moving around this issue of designated worship space, to the basics of worshiping God and being more concerned about Spirit and truth than place.

Sometimes we also get caught up in the physical details of our church life and miss the more important purpose for which we exist and gather as the people of God. At times, because of our histories at a certain place or a sense of loyalty to others who also are or have been there we just want to continue as we have done. Then we are not willing to look at what changes in attitude that may be necessary in order that we might worship better in spirit and truth.

In a congregation I served was a family who lived only a mile away from the church but only very rarely attended worship. One day there was a severe hailstorm that knocked out the windows of the building. Members of this family were the first to think of the church building and went over to see how it had fared through the storm. When they discovered that the windows were broken, they called the chairperson to report the damage and offered some money to pay for repairs. Because their forebearers had helped to put up the church building in their community they felt attached to it. There was a cemetery by the church where those relatives' bones laid buried. I expect that they felt that it was a holy place to them as well as a place of connection with previous generations and community. Somehow, they had missed the fact that what went on inside the church was more important than the building itself regardless of who had contributed it its construction and maintenance over the years.

The Samaritans continued to worship at Mount Gerizim where a temple was erected about 400 BC around the time of Alexander the Great. At that point in time, rebellious and outcast priests from Jerusalem provided service to the Samaritans. Later on in history, Israel was conquered by the Greeks whose thought and culture became a major influence on the Jewish society in Palestine and that process is called "Hellenization". In that era, the Greek thought and perspective also did affect the Samaritans. However, there has been a group of Samaritans who have continued even down to modern times in their tradition, long-steeped in a history of worshiping God based on the Torah only, not acknowledging the other writings of the Hebrew Bible as scripture.

Meanwhile, their Jewish neighbors in Judah had to mix with the gentiles when the majority of their population was taken into Babylonian exile. According to the prophets before this event, the reason for this deportation was that they had been practicing idolatry which they had accepted from their gentile neighbors. While both the Jews and the Samaritans were groups that were much concerned about cleanliness and purity, yet both had been affected by the impurity of gentiles who had invaded their lands and influenced them. The fallout of this gentile influence or suspicion about it, affected their attitudes toward one another.

There is a documentary on Netflix about the Silk Road and the influences that were brought west by the trading that happened because of those who used that route. When the early traders, firstly from the middle east, then later from Europe, made the long and challenging trek into China, they discovered all kinds of products that they brought back for trade in their homelands. These items were not known in the middle east or west at that time, items such as silk, paper, and gun powder. Furthermore, the traders also brought back ideas and systems of organization that were new to their own communities. So, the middle east and the west eventually were profoundly influenced by that interaction and trade between the west and east. Yet, Jesus was approaching alien territory and was shut out. Something far more important and helpful than even the silk road was lost because of the closed attitude of the Samaritan community that would not allow him even to visit there.

Throughout the life of the church, Christian disciples carried the message of Jesus out into the world where they also met rejection and resistance. Sometimes attitudes have changed, and doors were opened to let the light of Christ into their midst. This lesson reminds us of the importance of welcoming Jesus among us and to maintain a receptive spirit toward him and the Spirit.

It is helpful to consider how this alienation between the Samaritans and the Jews developed. Both the Samaritans and the Jews observe and keep the Torah and therefore have a common, basic text underlying their faith and practice. A major stumbling block to unity between these two groups was a dispute with one another over the central place of worship and the attitudes toward the background of each other.

The temple or the worship space was of utmost importance to both groups. The Samaritans worship at Mount Gerizim while the Jews worshiped in Jerusalem. The Samaritans maintained that when Israel was settled by the descendants of Jacob, the first place of worship was Mount Gerizim based on Deuteronomy 27:11. There they were commanded to make an altar and on Mount Gerizim was where six of the tribes of Jacob were blessed. They believe themselves to be from the blood line of Joseph and Judah was from the family of Judah. Instead of focusing upon their shared ancestors of Abraham, Isaac and Jacob they set the descendants from the different brothers as "the other" and as separate from themselves.

Attitudes toward others as differing from us, builds divisions and judgments between members in communities, congregations and even within families. The tendency is to then focus on the differences, whether real or perceived, and to allow alienation and misunderstanding to fester and further divide the group that could be working together for the larger good. Furthermore, such divisions can distract those who see themselves as distinct from those who are "other" in the process losing the central focus of Jesus to worship in truth and in Spirit. These distinctions and separation among us interfere with the greater desire of the divine for worshiping in the Spirit and in truth.

As a result, the intention of God for the people of God is lost amid the divisions. Perhaps we have a better chance of worshiping in truth and the spirit when we are together and able to learn from each other, practicing Jesus' challenge to love one another even those who we may see as the other.

This feels like a dispute that arises even in our families today when one member of the family feels more or less like they belong than others. When a member of a family feels that they are superior to others or are treated by the parents as more important than the others, the scene is set for a toxic environment. Then jealousy, resentment, competition, and hostility are generated. A case in point does go back to the story of Joseph who was favored by the father Jacob. That in turn led to major fallout between the brothers leading to Joseph's sale into slavery, and even the relocation of the family into Egypt.

While the place of Mount Gerizim was significant to the Samaritans, another place that became important during the early years when Israel was being divided and settled was Shiloh. In the text from Joshua, we hear that Shiloh had other significant meanings. In Joshua 18-21 the tribes of Israel gathered and the land was divided into the remaining parts of Israel at Shiloh for the tribes that had not been allocated territory. The tribes who had received lands on the east side of the Jordan decide to set up an altar there. The remaining tribes decide to make war against them because what they have done is thought of as a turning away from "the way of the Lord and building themselves an altar in rebellion against God" Joshua 22:16. Having a single central place of worship was thought to be a means of maintaining unity among the tribes of Israel.

In our society, where there are so many places of worship in most cities and towns, we might wonder why a place of worship became such a big issue. In Israel it had to do with the ark of the covenant as the most significant item to worship that was understood as the place where God dwelt most intensely. The ark of the covenant was understood to be the "seat of God" therefore it was the most holy object that made the dwelling in which it was housed also holy. Before any temple was erected, the ark was housed in a tent which moved with the people. Only when they settled did they build a more permanent structure to house the ark of the covenant and as such it became a central place of sacrifice and worship.

We can understand this perspective because our own places of worship also become holy places for us as well. It is here that we hear the word of God proclaimed, the sacraments are administered as well as the place where we sing praises to our God and lift our petitions for divine aid and praise. Our churches are places where we are blessed and nurtured or sometimes challenged by the divine, as such our places of worship do feel special and set apart for these holy purposes in relation to the Holy God whom we worship even though not in Israel.

To this day Jews and others gather to pray at the "wailing wall" which is part of the foundation of the temple mount in Jerusalem. Even though the ark of the covenant and the temple that housed it are long gone, there is a sense that that spot is still special and remains a place of contact with the holy.

The dispute about where the central worship place was to be arose and is associated with Eli the priest who raised Samuel. The Samaritans believe that Eli was responsible for the movement of the ark of the covenant from Mt. Gerizim to Shiloh. That became the site where the tabernacle was set up in the time before the monarchy was established in Israel. A grievance of the Samaritans is that they feel the importance of Gerizim was downplayed. Then, when the ark of the covenant was taken to Jerusalem and the temple built there, the Samaritans hold Eli, Solomon, Ezra, and Hillel responsible for making and keeping Jerusalem the central worship location for Israel. They feel that this decision was an apostasy or derivation from the way things should be and were at first. The Samaritans had the feeling that their perspective about this matter was not taken into account, and they reacted to what they saw as an error. No doubt this only deepened their sense of alienation from their Jewish neighbors and added to their sense of separation from them.

The Samaritans were not the only group that objected to the kinds of decisions made by leaders in Israel. Scholarly studies have revealed that there were a number of splinter groups before the fall of the Jerusalem temple in 70 AD. It sounds a little like the denominationalism that has grown up in North America.

The Samaritans asserted that they held to an earlier form of Judaism partly because they used only the first five books of the Bible and they claimed that the texts had been altered over the years by those worshiping in Jerusalem. This generated a spirit of suspicion and distrust in the Samaritans perspective against the Jews.

However, those who challenged the claims and viewpoints of the Samaritans questioned the purity of their theology because following the Assyrian conquest of northern Israel, the king of Assyria sent other groups to settle in the area of the Samaritans (2 Kings 17:24-27). These foreigners brought with them their pagan worship of other gods instead of worshiping the God of Israel. Then when people were attacked by lions, which was reported back to the king of Assyria, he thought that these attacks were because the people living in the area of Samaria were not worshiping the local god. Then he sent a priest who had been taken into exile from Jerusalem, to those living in Samaria with the mandate to teach them the worship the God of Israel. This history left a lingering sense among the Jews of the local people of the area of Samaria as being tainted by the idolatry of the foreigners who had been sent from Assyria to mix with them. This caused the Jews to view the Samaritans as polluted by the idolatry brought in by the foreigners that had settled there among the Samaritans. That in turn caused a sense of offense and judgment among the Jews toward the Samaritans.

The ironic thing is that there was cause to question the purity of the Jews who had gone into exile as well. The prophets before the exile repeatedly warned the Jewish people to turn away from the idolatries they had taken up from their contact with non-Jewish neighbors around them. But those warnings went unheeded. The days came when the Babylonian army invaded and took the majority of the people off to Babylon where they lived among the gentiles and were no doubt affected by that contact.

History has a way of continuing to affect attitudes, and to create a sense of being the chosen as opposed to those others deemed less fit to be equal. In the story of the history of Samaria one can see all kinds of judgments against those who had come from the same stock, which led them to being closed to others outside their one community. One has to understand the history sometimes to get a grip on what is causing conflict and negative attitudes of one group to another. The cost to these kinds of attitudes is that Jesus may walk by such communities, and they miss out on the more important gifts that he would bestow.

In the text from Luke 9:51-62 we see that Jesus did want to include the Samaritans in his good work and intended to go to them and make a visit there. There is encouragement in this intention. Even in the face of criticism, of hostility and rejection Jesus still desires to meet them and bless them as he did in other communities. In their insular state it is likely that this group had not heard of the wonderful work that Jesus was doing around them in other villages. In their unwillingness to offer Jesus and his disciples' hospitality, they would not hear from him and he walked by their community. Because he was headed for Jerusalem that was cause enough to close the door on him.

It is important that we cultivate a spirit of hospitality toward Jesus and those he sends us in his name. When we are receptive, he is able to come among us, and to us personally to teach, heal, care for and bless us. Our beliefs toward others and the behaviors that grow from those beliefs does have an effect upon the ability of Jesus to enter our lives and that of our community.

With open hearts we pray, "come Lord Jesus."

Amen.

Going So That The Kingdom Can Come

Have you ever experienced having to get something done, and of having a sense of urgency about accomplishing that task? Jesus is headed toward Jerusalem and has a sense of resolve to get done as much of the major work that he had come to accomplish before facing the ending of his life. He realizes that he cannot get it all done by himself and so he enlists seventy others to take up that great mission of his. However, in order to accomplish the mission of carrying the work and word out into the communities around there is need for some organization and personnel.

So many disasters have blighted the world over the past years. Images of them have been flashed across the screens of our televisions, computers and phones. There have been major earthquakes, and hurricanes or bombings from war that have reduced communities to rubble, killing many caught in the situation. Workers try to move debris in order to reach whoever may still be alive under it. Those scenes are chaotic and yet there are organizations prepared and ready to go into such places to offer aid, support and the basics of life to those who have been so affected by what has befallen them.

It seems in this text that Jesus had a sense that there was much to be accomplished, "the harvest was plentiful" and yet there were not enough workers to get the job done, "but the laborers were few, so ask the Lord of the harvest to send out laborers into the harvest."

In the text for today, we hear of Jesus doing just that. He gathered seventy workers and paired them up then sent them out, although they were not well-equipped for their work. In this world where there are so many disasters happening, and so much distress, even in settled communities needing workers to go out and do what needs to be done for the harvest. Furthermore, the time was pressing — as any farmer or gardener knows, the harvest needs to be taken in before the devastation of winter arrives.

One gathers from this passage the importance of having a mission or a purpose and goal before even starting out into the harvest. Then there is need to be ready and organized to move out into the work of collecting what waits and needs to be gathered.

A few years ago, my husband and I were invited to go and witness the harvest of a quarter section of land that had been sown with the intention of selling the harvest for the Canadian Food Grains Bank. The crop had been seeded by volunteer labor, seed, and equipment. Then later in the fall, farmers came with their combines to gather the grain that had been produced and was ready to be gathered and taken away to safe storage. The combines emptied their loads into trucks standing by, taken to the local elevator and sold. The proceeds of that grain sale were donated toward buying seed in another land closer to where there is need of food. That grain is then donated to those in need of it.

It was quite a sight to see. In that small field were about a half dozen combines and several grain trucks. Someone had spread the word about the date and time of this harvest. And the farmers came ready to get the job done. It only took them about a half an hour until they were finished and came from their combines to have a visit before taking their empty machines home with the job finished for another year. That is what happens when workers are well organized and when enough show up to work together for a good and larger purpose.

Here Jesus had enlisted seventy workers who were being sent out into a different kind of a harvest. Although they did not show up with combines and trucks they were sent out with a commission. When they entered a town, they were to heal the sick present and to proclaim that that kingdom of God had come near to them. All that rested on the hospitality of the members of the towns and villages where they were going. A prerequisite of accomplishing this important work was the openness and hospitality to those who had been sent to them.

Jesus sent these workers to prepare for what was yet to come, getting things ready for the day of the harvest. So too in the life of the church today there is a continuing need for those who organize and equip the ones who will be sent out into the harvest. A clear understanding of the message they were to carry and the capacity to provide healing as a sign of the wholeness and well-being that were part of the kingdom of God were also supplied.

That is an important part of the work of the church, the organizing, training, and sending that needs to be done to get the work of spreading the word of the kingdom. The better these jobs are done the better the work of tending to the great harvest can proceed. In addition, there is the challenge to appeal to the one whose harvest it is, to raise up more laborers. Those who organize cannot do their part of the work without those who need to be trained and sent out to particular ministries or fields for work. Where are the workers to come from? Pray, we are instructed, pray for owner of the fields to find and employ those who are needed to bring that harvest in. By grace, the owner of the fields can and does find and bring in those who are sent to work in the harvest. Yet it seems that there is need for us to keep asking for that grace and the working of the Spirit to provide the needed laborers for the great harvest.

In this text we see the power of the word and of healing are linked together in the commission of those Jesus sent out. There is still a great harvest even to this day that waits for the laborers to come and get to work. Are we not also a part of that group of laborers needed in the fields of human lives in this world? There is a sense of urgency about the work of harvesting because the produce or grain or forage needs to be brought in before it spoils or is lost to the weather. So too the harvest for the reign of God is also pressing, while there is opportunity and before the precious harvest is lost. We are needed to engage with those who are willing to receive us to share the good news and to work toward healing for their sake and the sake of the world.

The message carried out by those seventy was that the kingdom of God has come near. We hear this term, "kingdom of God" or "kingdom of heaven." What is really meant by these terms?

In Jesus' day it was expected that the kingdom of God would be ushered in by the Day of the Lord.

> Jesus also declares, "The kingdom of God is in your midst" (Luke 17: 21). Here and throughout the gospels, we discover that the reign of God breaking in and changing everything among us is *Jesus himself*. As John Timmer explains, "Just as Jesus' parables proclaim the kingdom of God, so does Jesus' life. His entire mission—his life, teaching ministry, death, resurrection, ascension—proclaims the kingly rule of God. The story of Jesus discloses to us a new way of living that is marked by total submission to the rule of God. ... At

the same time Jesus is both proclaimer and proclamation of God's regal rule" (*The Kingdom Equation*, 12).

"Kingdom," Eugene Peterson affirms, "is what Jesus reveals, patiently but insistently, word by word, act by act" (*The Jesus Way*, 21).[3]

The message in the text represents a scenario standing in contrast to the expected "Day of the Lord" as laid out in the writing of some of the prophets of ancient Israel. They set forth a vision of God coming with a lot of disturbance and signs accompanying the judgment the nations and their peoples before instituting the clear reign of God. Then the will and directions of God would finally be done by all, which will result in a wonderful time of peace, and prosperity, wholeness, and abundance for all the world. Whereas this teaching of Jesus is that the kingdom is among or within those who are hearing this message. The reign of God is present and lived among the ordinary lives of those who hear, receive the word, welcoming the one who spoke it and the message brought to them through those sent by Jesus.

What we have come to understand as the "Day of the Lord" or the day of judgment was a concept that developed over time among the Jewish people. In ancient Israel and among their neighbors in that area the belief was that each area and nation had their own local gods who had sovereignty over them. As a result, the rule and influence of those gods was limited to a certain group of people and their own area.

It was through the prophetic teachings of Israel that introduced the belief that there was one God who had influence over all nations and people. One can see how this understanding expresses the belief in monotheism, and that there is only one real God over all peoples and nations.

In the exilic and post-exilic period of Israel's history, the idea that God could use other nations or powers to accomplish the divine will grew. The prophets had warned Israel that they needed to change their ways and get back to worshiping their one and only God. Some of the prophets warned that if they refused to do this then their enemies would come and destroy their nation, their way of life, and take them into exile. And that is what happened. After they had been in exile for a number of decades the prophets foretold that another king would

3   https://www.thebanner.org/columns/2021/08/what-did-jesus-mean-by-the-kingdom-of-god-has-come-near

arise and conquer Babylon. He would then allow the exiles to return home with their sacred objects of worship.

King Cyrus did conquer and rule Babylon. He did in fact allow those who had been exiled to Babylon to return to their own lands with their sacred objects. Through the Jewish experiences that fulfilled the words of the prophets was gained a sense that God could and would use international leaders and circumstances to accomplish the purposes of the one true God of Israel, supported by their historical experience.

However, there was an ongoing issue with this kind of perspective in that other nations did not recognize or obey the will of this God, which led to continued suffering and oppression. This in turn led to the development of eschatology, or the study of end time things. That was based on the understanding that the rule and word of God is not yet totally heard or effective. Eschatology developed in response to the continuing presence and suffering caused by evil at work. In reaction to that, the prophets proclaimed that the day would come at some future time when God would be revealed clearly. Then people would finally believe and follow the will of the divine. Even as we pray in the Lord's Prayer, "Thy kingdom come, and your will be done, on earth as it is in heaven." The coming of that dominion of God in turn would usher in a golden age of peace, plenty and the good life when evil powers that oppose God would be overthrown once and for all.[4]

Connected with the coming of this kingdom of divine rule was that the Messiah would usher in the coming kingdom and rule of God. That hope has been a powerful dynamic especially when people find themselves caught in situations of injustice, tyranny, and bondage. The Jews at the time of Jesus were living under the rule and power, the domination of the Roman empire. The hope that the Messiah would come and set things right must have been a helpful belief to enable the Jewish nation to continue on in hope for a better future.

While the hope of the coming of the Messiah was important it was also forward looking. Jesus' message sent through the seventy is that the kingdom is already present with and within those who receive him who has come to set them free. It was an important message for the Jews at that time as well as Christians who find themselves experiencing suffering, injustice as well as losses caused by evil and unjust forces around them.

4   *Interpreter's Dictionary of the Bible An Illustrated Encyclopedia*, K-Q, vol.3 (Nashville: Abingdon Press, 1962) pp.17-26.

The day marking the initiation of the kingdom was expected to be one of power displayed and of judgment against the forces of evil. The instruction of Jesus for those being sent is quite the opposite to the expectation around the coming of the kingdom of heaven.

Instead of wielding swords and accompanied with fire and clashing thunder, Jesus sends his teams out at "lambs into the midst of wolves." They come gently and in vulnerability, without great displays of power and force, as he does when arriving in Jerusalem. He comes seated on a donkey welcomed by crowds not with swords, but with branches and clothes they lay on the road before him. As the ruler of this kingdom, he comes also as a lamb to face the injustice, the cruelty, the political maneuvering that were meant to take him down. On the cross, the Lamb of God gave up his life for those who belong to the kingdom and those in the world who would welcome him.

As we look at the instructions to those seventy in verse 4, we feel that they were sent out without resources to make their way in the world. They were to "carry no purse, (in other words, no extra money), no bag (no suitcase or duffle bag, or knapsack) to carry extra stuff, and no sandals. Let alone sturdy footwear for walking. Usually, we are better prepared for setting out on a journey, especially one that will require us to stay overnight.

I remember one time when I was young, I was working at a summer job in a hospital in a small town. My brother was working several hundred miles away on the railroad for his summer job. One long weekend he decided that he would come to see me but had no vehicle. He caught a ride from some other workers part of the way. Then he hitchhiked the rest of the way. He arrived with a summer jacket over his shoulder, and 25 cents in his pocket. He obviously trusted that he would be able to get to the town where I was and that he would be okay, which he was. Although he might have arrived rather hungry. But that is not the usual way that we go to visit our relatives for a weekend.

These instructions to the seventy implied that they would be provided for along the way, which required trust in the one who had sent them as well as others along the way. How many immigrants arrive in this country with very little? They too have set out in trust that they will make it through somehow. They too come needing the kindness, good will and hospitality of others along the way, even as most of our relatives arrived in this country as well.

The seventy set out in trust that they would meet hospitable persons who would receive them and provide for them. Such openness and receptivity are important elements to this campaign of bringing the kingdom near. The first thing that the sent are to do when they enter a house is to declare, "Peace to this house." Which is rather like testing the waters. How will those who dwell there respond? If they are people of peace that peace will rest on them. What a wonderful gift to bring to those who would open their house to these who are sent. However, if those in the house are not people of peace it will return to the one who offered it, so that peace is not lost.

The implication is that those who are to be healed and who will hear the message about the kingdom being near will only be able to receive it because of the presence of the persons of peace who welcomed these agents of Jesus. If these sent ones were not welcomed, they would leave brushing off even the dust of the town as they moved on. This illustrates how important that attitude of hospitality is to the work of the kingdom and the work of the laborers in the great harvest.

This attitude and gift is a vital part of Christian community! It was vital in Jesus' day, and it is just as needed these days. Even now we welcome the Christ into our communities, churches and our lives that indeed he might bring his wonderful kingdom within and among us. As he is present and is our leader, we begin to experience the peace and love that Jesus came to teach, to embody, and to share. We continue to welcome him and those whom he sends that the blessings of his reign may fill us and our lives aiding us to share this good news and our experience of it.

Furthermore, let us go forth to do our part in the work of Christ and in the great harvest that still requires all the workers' work and contribution. By the Spirit's guidance may we do our part in the gathering of the kingdom of God and the blessings granted in that realm.

Amen.

Rules Or Mercy

In Jesus day, a lawyer came to see Jesus with an important question on his mind. "What must I do in order to inherit eternal life?" Here was a person who was used to asking questions and seeking to get at the truth of various matters. I expect that this lawyer was a Jew who sought out Jesus to ask this question. If someone were to ask you this question, what answer would you give?

Jesus was clever in the way he approached answering the query from this person. Jesus answered this lawyer's question with a question, a good Jewish approach to such discussion. And Jesus sent him back to his own area of expertise in order to find the question. Jesus asked him, "What is written in the law? What do you read there?" In other words that answer to this question was already available in the written materials about the law at hand, and the lawyer does already know the answer to his question.

Sometimes aren't we similar to this lawyer? We, too, at times question what is written, or questions may arise for us even though we have read what the Bible has to say about these things. The lawyer came to test Jesus and sometimes, especially through times of testing for us, we too may question what we already know and wonder about what we have read or heard, or question whether there is something important that we have missed or not understood.

The lawyer answered Jesus question repeating the basic foundation of the law of God. The first part is that one is to love God entirely with all that we are. The first thing listed is to love God with all of the heart. For us when we hear this we think of the heart as the place associated with emotion, especially emotions of love, care, and kindness. This encouragement to love with the deepest of emotions is different than the Greek thinking intersecting with Jewish thought in Israel at that time. Greek philosophy believed that it was better to be detached from the emotions, to be dispassionate. Yet the Jews were told to love God with all your heart, with the entirety of the emotional part of life.

To engage with God in the fullness of emotion was being promoted in this law.

Furthermore, emotions were and are an important part of the understanding of God because emotion is a vital part of qualities and character of God and our relationships with the deity and others. While the Greek understanding of their gods was one of detachment and indifference to emotion. The Jewish view of the divine included a God who was full of compassion, mercy, and steadfastness, who was wanting to engage with people.

The feelings of love, mercy, kindness, and compassion as demonstrated in the parable of the Good Samaritan were emotions that were desirable and helpful in dealing with neighbors and are a reflection of the God who cares for all. When one's heart is cold and unmovable then such hearts are not likely to reach out to aid another in destress, and in fact the lack of caring response will show such people as not being a neighbor to others around them.

Our love of God is not a dispassionate business, but one that is closely connected to the heart and with the soul.

The second thing listed by the lawyer is to love God will all the soul. The soul in Hebrew is called the "naphesh." But how do we understand this word?

The website "Hebrew Word Lessons" has this to say about soul.

> **Your soul is YOU. It is Your Self.** It is what distinguishes you from everyone else around you. It is your uniqueness, your emotions and your reactions and how you view your life experience. Some may call it your essence. The truth is, you do not HAVE a soul… you ARE a soul.
>
> Think of your soul as **the very fiber of your being.** Check out the following verses that have the word *nephesh* and try substituting the words "every fiber of your/my being" in place of "my soul":

Deuteronomy 6:4

> *"Hear, O Israel! YHWH our God, YHWH is one! And you shall love YHWH your God with all your heart, and* **with every fiber of your being,** *and with all your might."*[5].

5 https://hebrewwordlessons.com/2018/02/04/soul-defining-nefesh-everything-you-wanted-to-know-about-the-soul/

Another way to look at this is to love God with who you are. Our relationships with the divine are not just following a set of rituals, or even just keeping a set of laws, regulations, or attending to duties but it is an engagement with the uniqueness of who we are with who God is thus undergirding a comprehensive kind of dynamic in the living of our daily life. And to answer the lawyers concern about inheriting eternal life. It is to live life within the context about love of God and neighbor which is intimately tied to faith in this one who loves us so completely, this then prepares us for continuing existence into eternity.

Some may ask, "How do we reach a place where we are able to love the God who loves us enough even to suffer and die for us in the person of Jesus?" 1 John 4:19 is instructive, "We love because he first loved us." The implication is that we are able to love God entirely because we are being loved totally by this one and only God. The love that comes from the divine returns to that source when we respond and love God with all of our soul, heart, mind and strength. In order to keep this part of the great command we require divine support and input. We cannot love God completely without the grace of divine love toward us.

There is a piece on the internet about a baby elephant whose mother was shot by poachers. Making her life even more difficult and adding to her loss, the herd rejected her. The game wardens in the area found her and took her to their sanctuary and named her Elly. They found that she was very malnourished and had some other health challenges. Eventually they did nurse her back to health, but she was listless and seemed terribly unhappy. Her keepers believed her to be depressed and wasn't doing well. They realized that she needed the herd. They took Elly back to her herd which only rejected her again. Now what were her keepers going to do to provide that community she obviously needed? They tried to introduce her to other herd animals in their care hoping someone would accept her into their group, but no other animals took her in and included her.

Finally, they introduced Elly to a mature, retired German Shepherd police dog, named Duma. Quickly they became friends and before long were inseparable. Duma taught Ellie how to play, which they did together for hours. These two animals also slept together and kept each other company through the days. Elly's mood improved dramatically.

In a way, the love, attention and interaction between the dog and the baby elephant became a lifeline for the Elly. That relationship was initiated by the dog who saw and understood that this little elephant needed and was willing to provide it for her.

Thank goodness the one who made us and cares for us every day of our life, also reaches out for us in love and understanding promising to never leave us nor forsake us. This command to love God with our entire soul reminds us that our relationship with the God who loves us so much is not a one-sided interaction, but the love of God calls us to respond in love with all that we are.

That challenge of the command also includes our strength, we are to love God with all our strength. How this is understood in Jewish thought is instructive.

After Moses' death, Joshua needed strength and encouragement as the new leader of Israel.

So, three times God encourages him with these words as he prepares to lead the nation into the promised land.

> The Hebrew word for strength — *chazak* — can also mean *courage*. In fact, courage is derived from strength — and not just physical strength.
>
> The Bible is full of instances of moral, spiritual, intellectual, and social strength that God expects his children to practice and excel at in our journey from glory to glory...
>
> After Peter and John healed a lame man in the name of Yeshua, the Sanhedrin (High Jewish Court) told them, "Stop it!" or they would undoubtedly face more imprisonment and flogging. Instead of withdrawing, the disciples banded together and prayed for strength and boldness to continue sharing the love of God and healing in the name of Messiah Yeshua:
>
> "And now, Lord, look at their threats, and grant to your servants to speak your word with all boldness, while you stretch out your hand to heal, and signs and wonders are performed through the name of your holy servant Yeshua." *(Acts 4:29–30)*

Following this prayer of unity, the place supernaturally shook.

> "They were all filled with the Holy Spirit and spoke the word of God with boldness." *(Acts 4:31)*

Sometimes we need to ask the Holy Spirit to refill us with strength. And sometimes, we need to ask others to band together with us in a united call for the Spirit's power to fulfill our mission.[6]

Strength is needed in order to accomplish things that needed to be done whether it is a physical job, or an administrative, or intellectual or emotional kind of work. If we are going to love God and neighbor well, we need the power to do it. Sometimes we need the strength of courage and persistence in order to even begin a much needed task such as carrying the gospel into our community or even family especially in that face of opposition and dismissal. We need courage but also wisdom in how to apply our strength. As a result, there certainly is need for the power of the Holy Spirit to accomplish the work and the call of God on our lives.

When I think of the work of Martin Luther, I am astonished by the amount of work that he accomplished in his life. He is certainly a historic example of someone who applied his full and considerable strength, courage, and stamina to work for the needed reformation of a large and dominant church of his day as well as deal with other voices that arose at that time of reformation. Martin Luther's life and strength was centered in his faith and service to God.

Some of us may struggle with the call to love God with all our strength because there are so many things that are calling for our strength, our capacities and even our courage. Our days are so full of the demands of daily life, long hours at work, followed by domestic duties at home, taking care of children or the elderly. We can feel that our strength is all spent in the daily round of our lives. How can we love God with all of our strength?

An important part of our love of God as well as our neighbors is in our service to them, which is our work. Our love gains expression through what we do with our time, energy, and resources. In the story of the Good Samaritan, he chose to stop and expend energy plus care on the man left beaten and robbed on the side of the road. But the Samaritan goes further than just physically helping the man on the side of the road. He also provides of his strength indirectly by supplying the money to keep him at the inn where he might have shelter and protection in order to recover. The funds provided were gained through the Samaritan's work, which he now supplies to the aid of a stranger in need of such "work" and support.

6 https://free.messianicbible.com/feature/be-strong-and-courageous/#:~:text=The%20He-brew%20word%20for%20strength%2

One time when I was a student, I was going to preach at a church that did not have a pastor at that time. It had snowed quite a bit the night before and the road was covered. It took longer than usual to get to my destination. When I was just a few miles from the church, I sped up a bit in an effort to get there on time. In a minute the back of the car swung around and was sitting in the deep snow of the ditch. Now what was I going to do? Worship was supposed to begin in fifteen minutes.

Then from the other direction came a three-ton truck with moose legs sticking out of the deck on the back of the vehicle which stopped. Four men hopped out of the truck crossed the highway and asked if I could use some help. With an immediate affirmative, they went around the car and practically lifted it onto the road. I certainly appreciated that act of strength that got me going again. I even arrived at the church with a few minutes to spare before the service started.

While what we do can be significant, it is important that we remember our strength and courage are dependent upon the sustenance and support supplied by the divine. While we are off spending our lives in various ways, they are meant to be supported by allowing God to direct us in the best uses of our powers. A vital part of our strength is to remain in touch with the God who is the source of all capacities and expend ourselves to the divine purposes and glory.

The parable of the vine and the branches speaks to this reality in our relationship with the divine. If we would live and thrive, it is necessary that we continue to receive the strength and nourishment that comes from the vine. We cannot do it by ourselves, nor are we intended to work alone without support and revitalization from the one who loves us and tends to us entirely. It is essential that we stay connected to the God from whom flows the strength and capacities that we need for this life and the service we render to others around us.

The third thing mentioned in this command to love God completely is to love God with our whole mind. The engagement of our minds in our devotion to our maker is not just about our emotional life, it also includes our intellect. Our thoughts, our perspectives, the way we make decisions and what we believe all are included in our full love of God.

In the story of the Good Samaritan, those who came along the road fall upon a traveler taking what he had and abusing him. These robbers' thoughts and perspectives were certainly not in line with the love of God. It showed how out of sync and destructive we can get when we are not loving God and neighbors.

Next was the thinking and decisions of those who also travelled on that road and their response to seeing the man on the side of the road. One wonders what their perspectives were as they walked on by the fellow lying by the road. The priest and Levite choose not to stop and provide assistance. They show that they are not neighbors of the man by the road either. They do not reflect the love of God. Obviously, their mind and thoughts were on other things, other fears, other pre-occupations.

The Good Samaritan saw the same thing as the two predecessors. However, how he thought about the situation was radically different. A spirit of mercy and kindness was linked to his thinking and pro-cessing of how to respond to the situation. He chose to offer aid, and to carry the man by the road to a place of shelter, safety, and comfort. The Samaritan also obviously thought about what he would do as he carried the man on his donkey. He planned out that he would get him into an inn, and that he would pay for his stay there from his own purse until he could return to take further action.

Our thinking is a vital part of how we live and the choices we make. It also affects how we see and understand what is going on around and within us. Recently I have been recovering from a surgery, a couple of friends made the choice to visit with me and arrived with flowers. Immediately I was grateful for their thoughtfulness and ef-forts to cheer me up.

I recently heard a comment from a speaker that sometimes when we are anxious, or discouraged, or feeling badly about ourselves, it has to do with how we understand what is going on around us, and our thoughts about our situation and ourselves in it. He went on to say that when we are feeling these difficult things, it is time to return to God seeking the divine perspective, and way of seeing things. Even though we are beloved of God, who has taken measures to care for us now and always, and has forgiven us, we can lose sight of these truths. Then we get caught up in thought patterns which can steer us off track so we focus on that which negatively affects us and our sense of self, making our lives difficult and stressful.

Loving God with all of our mind is crucial, and again we need God's perspective to help us to turn to the mind of our heavenly par-ent, Jesus and the Spirit so that we will come to more fully know the truth and walk in it. So much depends on our thinking, and even more depends on the mind of Christ. As we seek to love God with our whole self, let us seek the mind of Christ and his perspective to fill our minds, our hearts, while guiding our strength enabling us to love our blessed triune God ever more fully and with all that we are and all that we have.

Like the lawyer who came to Jesus seeking the path to eternal life, we also are challenged to love God with all of our heart, with all our soul, with all our strength, and with all our mind, and to love our neighbor as ourselves. May we ever turn to God seeking the divine perspective, power, and love to enable us to more fully live in love of our triune God and our neighbors.

Amen.

Proper 11 (16)
Luke 10:38-42

Host Or Guest?

Who is being host to whom in this story of Jesus' visit with Martha and Mary?

Martha was the more hospitable and maybe the more outgoing sister who welcomed Jesus into the home of Lazarus, Mary and herself. As he travelled around, Jesus likely did need and appreciate the hospitality of others who would invite him into their homes. Martha was sensitive to his practical need for nourishment, and set about attending to that provision. She was focused on offering hospitality and food so that her guest would feel cared for and welcome. That is what would be expected of someone inviting another into their house.

In the challenge to love our neighbors as ourselves, a part of that is the work of service. How much good work is done in community by those who are willing to roll up their sleeves and do what needs to be done for those who are in need? Sometimes we read or hear about important charitable projects that are being conducted by people of good will to improve the lives and state of others.

Recently there was a news item in which Israel was being encouraged to allow greater aid to enter Gaza. On May 2, 2024, an announcement was made on the news that the state of Israel was opening a gateway into Gaza to allow more aid to flow into the country. And there are agencies and individuals who will gladly move through that gate with their trucks filled with needed supplies for those who are starving and thirsty, as well as those with medical needs in Gaza. Thank goodness for the goodwill and preparedness to serve that is reflected in those acts of kindness and provision.

It seemed straightforward to Martha. When one has a guest then one has to treat the guest in the accustomed manner. Likely there were expectations around such hospitality. One can read about a similar expression of middle eastern hospitality when a couple of angels showed up at Abraham's tent. Before long he acted like Martha in this story and ran off to see that a hot meal was prepared for these unexpected guests. It seems that there was a long history in that area about how one treats guests. As a consequence, Martha got exasperated with her sister who was sitting there in the front room instead of busy getting things ready to serve the guest. Martha's expectations of her sister probably were handed down through tradition. While she swung into action and focused upon preparing a meal for their guest she wanted her sister there in the kitchen with her.

Martha welcomed Jesus into the house and felt that she needed to prepare a meal for him, in anticipation that he would be hungry. Her intention was good. It was also attached to her expectations as a host to a guest.

Don't we also approach situations with expectations of all kinds? We have a sense of the way things ought to be or should be done. We also have expectations of ourselves. Where do these perceptions about ways of behaving, or of anticipation are based upon our past experience, or behaviors and responses as patterned by others who we are looking to for as models of acceptability? Isn't that part of the whole glamour industry? There is also strong pressure on children and youth to wear certain kinds of clothes, and their hair in ways that will help them to fit in with the group and be acceptable.

We also have expectations about ourselves sometimes instilled by our families that we will conform to their ways of being together, or our parents may have had hopes for our lives which we might accept or rebel against, either way those expectations have a significant impact on our lives and futures.

Sometimes, those expectations can be helpful at other times they can be like an automatic response that may cause us to miss something else that is even more important than acting in the usual fashion.

There was a new boy in school who was feeling awkward and on the edge of the group. Because he had not been a part of the group he was left on the sideline and ignored. He was what could be called a nerd, and even as time went on, he did not feel like he belonged. There was one person in the group who took an interest in this newcomer and reached out to connect with him, inviting him to join in a game after school. The offer was accepted, and it was the beginning of a friendship — one that would last through the rest of their school years and beyond. Sometimes social prohibitions prevent what would be important and maybe even life changing interactions that could add considerable value to one's life. On the other hand, there are times when social restraints might protect especially vulnerable persons from being taken advantage of or led astray. Wisdom and discernment are needed in our relationships with social and public settings.

Sometimes we have expectations of ourselves and because of what we believe about ourselves and our place in family and community, we get stuck there and miss out on moving in a new and helpful direction. How many lack confidence and expect that they could not successfully negotiate a change? Then for fear of failure or of being unaccepted in new circles they do not explore different options?

There was once a person who felt that she could not do anything new other than what she knew and stayed mostly in her home. She got involved in her children's school as a volunteer. The staff there were wonderful and encouraged her, expressed appreciation for her efforts, and gave her feedback about her positive qualities as well as her strengths. The time spent volunteering in that school had a positive impact on her life. She found a job which brought much needed income into the home and gave her some independence. It also built her up in confidence.

In this text before us today, Martha greeted Jesus and had strong expectations of herself, her sister, and the situation around Jesus' visit. She acted on those expectations and was removed from dialogue with Jesus while she worked in the kitchen. When she complained to Jesus about her sister's absence and lack of help in food preparation, she discovered he had other expectations. He had an entirely different perspective about his visit to these sisters. As reflected in his comment to her: "Martha, Martha, you are worried and distracted by many things; there is need of only one thing. Mary had chosen the better part, which will not be taken from her." I am sure that stopped Martha in her tracks and helped her to set aside what she was doing in the kitchen to join Mary in listening to Jesus.

This is a challenging message in our age where there is so much to do, so many expectations to meet about a multitude of needs and demands. As we try to handle it all, that busyness can and does interfere with the more important thing. It takes time and a conscious decision sometimes to set aside the other obligations, or to prune them down to basics. Sometimes it helps for us to make the decision to set aside other things that keep us busy and distracted with the lesser things. This text lifts up how important the act of being present and listening to Jesus and also to others around us.

I read a brief comment by a person about their upbringing. This person felt that they had a wonderful childhood. Their mom in particular was there for her kids. She spent time reading to them and doing things with them. When they came home from school, she wanted to know what they had learned that day and what had happened. The grown-up child admitted that the house was a mess sometimes because their mom was doing other things with the kids. But in the bigger picture, the child appreciated that she and her siblings were a priority over housework. She felt her mom's attention and involvement in her life as a youngster had been so significant in who she had become and appreciated the many happy memories she had of the time in her life.

There is an epidemic of loneliness in our western nations. How much has that been created by busyness and distractions? This has resulted in the lack of time and space in our lives and schedules in order to stop and really listen, especially to Jesus but also to others around us.

There was a pastor who also had been a social worker living in Calgary, Alberta, Canada, who had a heart for the poor and homeless people loitering and living downtown. He expressed an interest in working with this population and the congregation agreed to support him in a part time ministry there. In the beginning, Pastor Ray would go downtown and sit on a bench in the area where the homeless and poor would be hanging out. He took with him a pack of cigarettes and lighter. He sat there for a number of weeks before some of those around would join him on the bench, maybe asking for a cigarette that he provided. That often would begin a conversation. Eventually he and those speaking to him moved to a restaurant in the area where he became well known. Pastor Ray was present and obviously had time and a willingness to hear those who came to talk. Over time, he became more involved with a ministry to those who simply needed a good heart, a listening ear as well as someone to encourage and support them. He became quite well-known to that community in the shadow of the skyscrapers and the large corporate office to those who lived in the shadows below. So, who needs us to slow down, and listen?

Furthermore, it is even more important that we slow down and intentionally listen to Jesus and what he has to share. In this lesson of his visit with Martha and Mary we can come to understand that when he is present with us it is most important that we sit with Mary and Martha, pay attention to him, and listen to him. We need to know that being with Jesus *is* the priority. If we allow other things, even worthwhile things, to push us away from listening to him what will we miss when we do not attend to the word speaking to us and our hearts?

While Martha wanted to offer good hospitality to Jesus, it turned out that Jesus wanted to offer her his hospitality and the single most important and needed thing that came from himself, his presence, and his point of view. Did he come needing a good meal and conversation with these two women or did he come expecting to share his message and companionship with them? This visit with the sisters was an opportunity for Jesus to come into their home to spend time with them and to be present with them as a way for him to care for and provide for them. In that way, Jesus became the host as he shared himself and what he would communicate.

This text aligns with the emphasis on the importance of the words spoken in the word of God. Through the power of that word working with the Holy Spirit, we are enabled to have faith in the one who came to visit Martha and Mary and to speak to them his precious word. By grace our hearts, minds, and ears can be opened to what he has to say to us. Even as those who are Jesus followers do we access that word and his perspective enough?

There are so many voices and projects, so many responsibilities and things that we feel we have to do that it is easy for us to feel completely consumed with it all. We come to the end of the day or week feeling fully spent. In that context, there is so little room or sense of being present for anything else and it is easy to not have room to invite Jesus in to spend some time sitting with him and listening to him as well as enjoying his wonderful companionship with us.

One Sunday at church, one of the regular attenders had taken a seat close to a pole in the church. As I was preaching, I noticed him nodding off. After the service I mentioned his snooze during the service. He explained that was the reason for sitting behind the pole — hoping that if he did doze off it would not be noticed and he then went on to tell me about his life at that point.

He had worked a lot of overtime over the previous few weeks, and then had to take his boys to tournaments all day Saturday, and the rest of Sunday. He was simply exhausted. In the face of all that

I could understand how he had nodded off but appreciated that he had made the effort to attend church in the face of his great weariness. Even though he missed the sermon, hopefully his power snooze did refresh him somewhat. For many, life is just too busy. There are so many expectations others have of us or we have of ourselves that fills up our time, our energy, and our space. There are times when we too need Jesus to arrive at our "house" — our reality — and knock on our door. Will we let him in and sit to engage him in conversation or to be engaged by him — or are we too busy and are running off to get something else done?

In this age, it is easy for us to get caught up in a lifestyle or way of thinking about things that is not helpful to us, and may drag us down. Jesus wants us to have a life of abundance and wellbeing. He came to provide that for us through living with him and attending to his word. Furthermore, he wants us to have the peace that only God can give. How do we get there? It helps for us to turn to Christ with what is on our hearts and minds, honestly speaking about these things. Sometimes we come to believe things that are not true even about ourselves or our lives because of what we have been through.

The truth remains that we are precious in Jesus and our heavenly parent's eyes, and they want us to know that we are valued and wanted. Jesus desires coming to us as well to keep us company and to speak his truth to our hearts, minds and lives. However, he cannot bring all these marvelous benefits to us if we are "not home" or not available because we are totally occupied with other things. Those things may be not only in the kitchen but in other places or states of mind that occupy us with many things.

Isn't it wonderful that Jesus does want to come and be with us? Isn't it a blessing to know that he would come to listen and to speak to us, our hearts, minds and lives? Jesus has time and attention for us no matter what else is happening in our lives. For our own good, he may have to challenge us like he did with Martha to come away from our busyness to spend time with him and with others who are gathered with him, eager to receive what he has to offer us. Jesus comes and wants to connect with us, to have a close relationship with us as a good friend whom we are glad to welcome into our homes and to freely share what is on our minds and hearts.

Sometimes we can lose sight of these important truths about the feeling that God has toward us, and we can lose sight of our place in the presence of the divine. Things can happen to us when we are treated without regard or respect so that we may come to feel that we are not valued or wanted. We may feel cast aside, or rejected or overlooked or that someone or a system is taking advantage of us. These things can leave us feeling that we have no worth.

While we may feel this way, in Jesus and our heavenly parent's eyes we have great worth. God wants to have us close to the divine heart free to be who we are to share all the things that are on our minds and hearts. Then too to hear God's perspective about us, and to come to know the truth of God's wonderful love and complete care for us regardless of what the world or others around us would say or do.

We are precious in the eyes of God. We are so loved and valued that God in the person of Jesus has entered into the pain of this world, and even into death for our redemption and life now as well as forever. In the person of Jesus, the divine would enter into our homes, and hearts to bring the truth of Christ's great compassion and companionship with us. So, the question arises: do we open our homes and hearts to him and seek his point of view? Is Jesus welcome into our lives and points of view? Do we seek the words of Jesus to us? Do we have a sense that there is a place at the feet of Jesus for us too, and Jesus is welcoming us to join him there?

In truth, the words of Christ are a priority, and they bring us life, health, and salvation. However, like Martha and Mary, it is vital that we welcome him into our lives and our condition that he might bless us through himself.

Amen.

Ask

Aren't we glad that the disciples asked Jesus to teach them to pray? Through Jesus' provision of this form of prayer, we also are able to use it even today and receive the benefits of it. The disciples saw Jesus withdrawing to pray. He was a practitioner of prayer and as such he provided a model for his followers.

Obviously, prayer was a vital part of Jesus' powerful ministry and preparation for what was to come in his journey through this world. The disciples wanted to be able to pray like him especially as they sought to follow him and to do the work that he sent them out to do. They would need to be able to pray like Jesus if they were going to follow him well. If they were to be able to take up their cross and follow Jesus, they too would need the power of prayer to enable them do that.

The disciples, like Jesus, required the power of prayer to take up their charge of carrying the message of Jesus to the ends of the world. They would go into areas and situations where that gospel and its bearers would be rejected, treated harshly, even killed as Jesus was. The disciples, like Jesus before them, required the assistance, the direction, the strength, and the connection with the God who sent Jesus. Prayer would be an avenue to gain divine support, strength, and care in order to carry out the mandate Jesus would entrust to them. The disciples proclaimed as well as witnessed to the power of Christ to overcome all that would separate us from God through his work on the cross and in the resurrection.

As Jesus and his disciples had to have the practice of prayer as part of their lives and mission, so we in this age also require a solid prayer connection. How vital is that avenue of communication with the one in whom we trust to grant us forgiveness, life now and into the future. The Lord's Prayer is a good beginning to the practice of prayer. Although there certainly is room for us to grow in our capacity to pray, it is also important for us to listen to and receive what God will grant. As we engage in the important work of prayer, our faith, our trust, and devotion to our triune God can deepen and grow in depth so that we can better face what life brings us. The closer we grow to the one who formed us, who redeemed us and keeps us for all of the future, the more we can enter in divine joy and celebrate the marvelous love that brought Jesus to us, and bestowed the Spirit upon us.

Quite a while ago, a bishop from the Coptic Church of Egypt was asked to address a gathering of clergy. He spoke about that church, its history, and its experience in the nation of Egypt. One of the challenges that the Coptic Church of Egypt has dealt with through the centuries, has been persecution from other religions, especially Islam. The Coptic Church and their practice of withdrawing into the desert for prayer and fasting has been a vital source of strength, endurance, and faith, which the bishop claims has enabled the Coptic Christianity to survive and continue through the ages into the present. Based on their confidence in prayer, their experience with its power, provides them courage and stability to face into whatever challenge comes next along their way. They have learned as a community to rely on the power of prayer and fasting to keep them enduring, strong in faith, and trust in order to weather through whatever opposition and obstacles they encounter individually or as a church community.

When asked to teach the disciples to pray, Jesus doesn't set up a six-week seminar on prayer — although that can be a helpful exercise and opportunity for growth in the capacity to pray. Rather he provided the simple form of what we now call the Lord's Prayer, which is being used by Christians of various denominations to the present day. It can also be a shared form of prayer within a church community.

The giving to his disciples this form of prayer was an expression of Jesus' work as rabbi. He was responding to a request and was teaching based on the tradition of Jewish patterns, thought, and practice. So, as we pray this important prayer, we too are following the teaching of rabbi Jesus. We thank God for this basic prayer as a way to connect with the divine, which is a vital part of our life of faith. It is also a means of requesting what we continue to require every day, accompanied with praise of the one whose name is holy. In addition, this prayer is available for us to say together as part of community in our worship life. It is an expression of our shared faith as a part of the church and is shared across denominational expressions of the Christian faith. As a form of prayer that we can pray together, it can bring a sense of unity and participating together in an important act, which can be helpful.

One time a pastor told a story about being called to the home of a grieving family that had just received news about the unexpected and violent death of a family member. Those gathered were in a state and there was a sense of chaos and commotion in the room. The pastor asked everyone to join in saying the Lord's Prayer. That act of focusing and participating in saying the Lord's Prayer helped to settle the group so they could move on to some helpful conversation.

What a blessing it is to have this simple yet concise prayer to share as well as to use individually in our worship. When we ask for the basics and offer praise to our great God who hears our every prayer and attends to us. How glad we are that the disciples did ask Jesus to teach them to pray so that we too could receive this gift of the Lord's Prayer for our life of discipleship as well.

Many of us pray the Lord's Prayer every day. But where did this form of prayer come from or did Jesus come up with it there on the spot?

This form of the Lord's Prayer drew from an earlier form of prayer in Judaism known as the *"Amidah"*, or the *"shemoneth esrah'*. It was known as the "Standing Prayer" that was prayed standing and facing Jerusalem. Some of the parallels between the *Amidah* and the Lord's Prayer include, for example, "Hallowed be thy name" relates to the third *Amidah* blessing: "Thou art holy and thy name is holy…We will sanctify thy name in the world, as thy sanctifiers in the heavens above… And forgive us our sins, for we ourselves forgive everyone indebted to us," relates to the fourth *Amidah*: "Our Father, Our king, forgive and pardon all our sins."[7] The Lord's Prayer is a much simplified form of prayer compared to the *Amidah* prayer.[1.]

In the New Testament there are two versions of the Lord's Prayer, one in Luke and one in Matthew. The big difference between the two is that the Matthean text includes the final word of praise. The Lukan form of the Lord's Prayer seems rather truncated. In the *Amidah*, the final section includes these words, "May the expression of my mouth and the thoughts of my heart find favor before you, Hashem, my rock and redeemer" and these words echo Psalm 19. They seem to be a good way to end such a prayer.

---

7   https://www.workingpreacher.org/commentaries/revised-common-lectionary/ordinary-17-3/commentary-on-luke-111-13-5#:~:text=Luke%20encou; Shemoneh Esreh – Biblical Cyclopedia," *Mcclintock and Strong Biblical Cyclopedia.* n.d., accessed May 7, 2022, https://www.biblicalcyclopedia.com/S/shemoneh-esreh.html.

The Levites took care of things connected to the temple worship, the rites, and the rituals included in the temple worship. The rabbis' work included answering the questions asked in the Jewish community and offering direction about how to interpret and apply the commandments and teachings. The rabbis would discuss among themselves the various ways to understand and apply what was in the Torah. In the gospel of Luke, this prayer is given in response to the request of the disciples of Jesus that he teach them to pray was part of his work as a rabbi. Even in Jerusalem while the temple was still standing, there were about 480 synagogues during the time of Jesus. The temple worship and synagogue were both active in the lives of the Jewish people at that time.

As part of the work of a rabbi, Jesus would instruct his disciples in the prescribed prayers and rituals that were to be practiced daily by faithful Jews. Here we see him teaching his disciples this brief but important prayer. In the early Christian writing called the *Didache* and those reading it are encouraged to continue the practice of praying the Lord's Prayer three times daily.

In the sharing of this important prayer with the disciples it has been passed on to us, the disciples of Jesus even to this day. As a result, we as gentiles have access to this vital prayer provided by Jesus based on the earlier forms of prayer in Judaism. It is a part of worship in the liturgy of the church. Since the time of the early church the Lord's Prayer is usually said prior to receiving the elements of holy communion.

Following the words of the Lord's Prayer, the text shifts to talk about the nature of the one to whom the prayer is addressed. This prayer is addressed to "Our Father in Heaven". This defines who we are praying to, and from whom we expect an answer to these petitions. The question arises about what kind of a Father is being addressed here? What follows the Lord's Prayer provides clarification about the nature of the one who is being addressed. In so doing we are being taught about the nature of our heavenly parent.

The first analogy is that of someone coming to ask bread for guests arriving late in the night. While it would be understandable that those being asked would not want to bothered by such an inconvenient request when they are already in bed. But because of the relationship of friendship between the one asking and the one being asked, that person would get up and provide what is being requested.

When we come to ask of God what we need, no matter what the time or circumstances, we will be heard and attended to because of the care and the close relationship with us as the "friends of God". We are free to ask for what we need when we need it, the divine ear and heart is available to attend to us at any time of the day or night. Even as parents of babies, we have to be willing and able to get up at night to attend to the cries of their little ones for food or care.

One time there was no food in the house where Mother Teresa lived with her community. However, at the mealtime, she called the community to the table though there was nothing on it. She began to pray thanking God for what would be provided. After a while there was a knock at the door. When it was opened there stood a man with a sack of rice on his shoulder as a gift to the community living in that house.

As the door was opened by the friend in the house for the friend outside, we are encouraged to ask for what we require. "Knock and the door will be opened for you." Isn't that a wonderful invitation, especially for those who have to deal with a lot of closed doors that will not be opened regardless of how long they knock?

In this time when there seem to be so many needs and so much anxiety about whether we will be able to get the necessities because of instability in the economy and the world, it is so good to know that God is there for us. We are encouraged to knock on the divine door through our prayers, for others and ourselves. Someone once said that he did not think that he should need to pray for what he needed because God who knows all things knows already. He believed that God knew what was needed and it was up to the divine to provide it one way or another. However, it seems that there is a desire from God that we do approach and knock on God's door seeking to engage with the divine concerning our needs. And maybe some things are not given because they are not requested. The text seems to indicate that sometimes we need to seek and ask for that which we need. Our prayers are a means of opening doors not only for ourselves but for others as well. Prayers and intercessions are important avenues of communication and interactions between God and us.

I remember one time when talking to someone about prayer, she said that she did not ask for what she desired in prayer because it seemed to her to be a selfish thing to do. Yet this text seems to tell us that God is waiting for us to seek for what we require or desire from God and to ask for it. As we pray for these things, it is an expression of our awareness that we do depend upon God rather than just upon ourselves and our own capacities. In our relationship with the divine that is important. We are encouraged to seek for what we need, and to request it. Then, when it is provided, we can recognize the hand of God in attending, and caring for us.

One thinks of the many parents and guardians in the world are not able to supply their children with even the basic necessities. That inability would be another significant part of the suffering in that situation of hunger, or thirst or homelessness. This reminds us of the importance of seeking and providing support for those who are facing hunger, famine and having no shelter. We may be the avenue through which God is answering prayers of parents and children in need.

The next item mentioned in the text is when a child asks for a fish or an egg. Obviously, a loving parent will provide the youngster with as good food as they possibly can. God as a parent is generous and will attend to the needs of the child. The question is asked which person when asked by a child for fish will instead give a snake? God is not malicious and mean but will respond with generosity and appropriately for the well fare of those who are asking. We can trust the goodwill of the heavenly father.

A few years ago, the Canadian Lutheran World Relief was asking for donations for fish nets. They were to be sent to an area that usually was a desert. However, with the sudden inundation of an unexpected rainfall, the area flooded and suddenly fish were abundant. With the fish nets, those who were hungry could fish for some food and gain some needed protein in their diet. Maybe there were some who were asking for fish in that area prior to that flood.

Following this example of fish is a similar kind of request but for an egg. Which parent would give a scorpion instead? That would just be mean, and so contrary to the love parents hold for their children.

The obvious answer is no parent would do such an unkind thing to their own children.

The line of thought in this portion of text continues on that even those who are evil know how to give good gifts to their children, how much more will the heavenly Father give the Holy Spirit to those who ask! Beyond the physical and emotional aspects of life for which we pray, God desires to grant us the Holy Spirit who provides wonderful attributes and spiritual blessings. And God as parent wants to give us this significant gift that keeps on giving, yet in order to receive these blessings it is important that we ask for the Spirit.

The Holy Spirit is the avenue through which God provides the connections with the Trinity that are so vital for our faith and connection to the divine. Firstly, through grace and the power of the word the Spirit enables us to become children of our heavenly parent who cares for us so much and tends to us. How can we approach the divine as our heavenly parent if we do not belong? The Spirit comes when the door is opened to the Spirit through our requests of her presence in our lives. The Holy Spirit is a major gift and means of provision granted to us through the love and care of the divine. We only enter into relationship with God as parent and provider through the working of the Holy Spirit and the word of scripture.

Furthermore, Jesus taught that the Holy Spirit is an advocate and helper especially in relationship with the other members of the Trinity. What an important gift and provision to have the Spirit given to us so that we can pray with the aid and intercession of the Holy Spirit. In the faith given by the Holy Spirit we can speak and listen as those who have been enabled to become children of the heavenly parent who attends to us.

Affirming that God wants us to approach the divine, seeking to communicate with trust in the unending goodness and generosity of our heavenly Father we continue to use the Lord's Prayer as part of our daily lives and worship. Yet we do not stop there, rather we continue to knock on the door of God's presence and attention seeking what we most desire, even the deeper communion and blessing of the divine in the gifts of the Holy Spirit, and a strengthening of our faith.

Amen.

Proper 13 (18)
Luke 12:13-21

What Kind Of Wealth?

Dr. Paul Trudinger shared: "One night I was deeply moved by a segment shown on the TV news, in which a man, an East Indian by birth, and his wife were being interviewed. This man, whose name I cannot recall, was born into, and brought up in poverty in New Delhi. As a child he frequently slept on the streets and scrounged his food from garbage cans. He had the spirit, however, to want to make something of his life, and eventually he migrated to Canada and settled in the Vancouver area. From small beginnings in business, he gradually built up a large real-estate operation and became a large property owner and a multi-millionaire.

The interview was held on the occasion of he and his wife's announced decision to give away almost all of their assets, putting them into a trust account to be used to help poor people in the Third World countries to improve their lot and get a start toward a more fulfilling life. He said that his past wealthy lifestyle began to give him little or no satisfaction and became a burden to them both. As his wife said: "We don't need four or five cars, several residences, dozens of pairs of shoes, and so forth." He said that they had come to learn that life's spiritual values were far more important to them than the material ones they had been living by." [8]

This is the opposite kind of a story than the one told by Jesus in the gospel text before us from Luke 12: 13. In the encounter between the person wanting an alteration in the distribution of a family inheritance and the request was made that Jesus intervene and divide the residue of another's life differently.

This individual was not wanting to give what was available but obviously wanted more of it. Jesus refused to get involved in this

8 Paul Trudinger, *Indirections To God: A Book of Reflections* (Winnipeg: Greenwood Place Publications, 1991), p. 35.

kind of situation. Instead, he warned of the dangers of greed and of wanting extra. Jesus warned that there was a danger in the wanting of more and more. In our society there are many who would dismiss this warning of Jesus in the dedicated pursuit of gaining more. These folk would argue that more is better because of the perceived benefits of having more wealth, more properties, more material stuff.

Following his interaction with the person wanting him to help him get more of the family inheritance, Jesus shared a parable of the farmer who had to deal with getting more in the harvest and the consequence of his attitude as a result of that abundance. The farmer built bigger granaries in which to store all that additional grain. Then when his new and bigger granaries were filled, he felt that he now could take it easy and enjoy life. That could become the goal of life, to have plenty so then one can "enjoy life" doing what we want. There is an element of freedom in having plenty, freed from scarcity and anxiety about getting what one needs or desires. In addition, many feel that in having wealth there is a sense of security, of status, and of power. While there are benefits to having an abundance there is the danger of how much wealth can affect how we view and treat others. Furthermore, it can interfere with our relationship with the true God of all who has provided life itself and all that is necessary for it.

Margaret Halsey made this observation about being so focused on money and things, "A commercial society urges citizens to be responsible for things, but not for people." This perspective has considerable impacts on relationships not only of individuals but on the society as a whole.

Jennifer Welsh provided an analysis about the growth of the ultra-wealthy and the impacts of that trend on society in her lecture on the Canadian Broadcast Corporation (CBC) program called *Ideas*.[9]

She spoke about the growing inequality between the ultra-wealthy and the general population. While the rich are getting richer the ordinary citizens are experiencing a continuing drop in purchasing power. One example of this is that in the past most citizens were able to buy a house, but currently the prices have skyrocketed. It has become impossible for many people to even think about owning their own homes, even as the rents take more and more of their incomes. The rising cost of the basics such as food is a growing concern especially for those who live on lower incomes. They have less while the prices continue to climb, and the profits of the food chains climb ever higher.

9   Jennifer Welsh, Part three of Massey Lectures; *Ideas*/CBC, May 10, 2024

Jennifer Welsh continued on to talk about the effect of this great wealth in the hands of the few in relation to the issue of equality in society and democracy. Democracy has as a fundamental stance that all citizens are valued and have an equal right to participate in the political arena. However, with the growing chasm between the very rich and the rest of the population there is a shift toward the wealthy gaining more power in the political and economic spheres. This has given them more influence which is utilized to affect the decisions made to benefit themselves instead of the common good. Therefore, the concern, perspectives and influence of the other citizens are curtailed thus eroding the working of democracy. Furthermore, in a study concerning the attitudes of the wealthy toward others it revealed a growing lack of compassion toward others, and a sense of entitlement to their wealth accompanied by a lacking sense of responsibility for others.

This program spoke about the dangers, including the spiritual dangers of having a life filled with the material wealth of society. The love of neighbor and the love of God gets lost, when one's life becomes totally engrossed in the stuff and powers of this world.

To this situation we hear Jesus' warning, "Take care! Be on your guard against all kinds of greed; for one's life does not consist in the abundance of possessions." Be on your guard against greed, the wanting and pursuit of more and more. It raises the issue for us about how much is enough for us?

A chaplain in a seniors' home saw the reality of this demonstrated in the lives of those he met while serving there. Some residents during their lives had accumulated all kinds of things that they needed or enjoyed. But as they grew older, they were not able to care for it all, or had reached a point where their health would not permit them to continue doing what they had done before. Because of the effects of aging, they found it necessary to let go of what they had. How many garage sales hold the things of those who are downsizing? Finally, following these dispersals of their goods, some have found themselves with only a few personal possessions living in single room in a care facility while others have bought or received what they previously had owned.

While there are so many attractive things for us to buy or to own in our society, we only have them for a time. These things, no matter how much we want or enjoy them, we will possess only for a while, and they will not last nor belong to us forever. Even while we must invest part of our lives in the accumulation of what we need for life in this world, we are wise not to totally invest ourselves in the things of this life, nor the pursuit of them. There is something even more important hidden amid all the shops, the entertainments, and the cupboards and closets of this life. In fact, all this stuff may obscure that which really does give us peace, and security, namely God.

If we would be truly rich then we need to look beyond the stuff of this world which is passing. Even as our lives are not a permanent part of this world, neither are we able to permanently possess what we acquire and own here either. The purpose of life is about something more than the accumulation of wealth and things. That alternate possibility raises a challenge about the priorities of our lives.

The punchline of this conversation between the family member and Jesus comes after he tells a parable about a farmer with a good harvest who builds more granaries and then thinks that he can relax, eat, drink and be merry for many years. Jesus in verse 20-23 Jesus concluded with, "This very night your soul will be demanded of you and all the things you have prepared whose will they be? So, it is with those who store up treasurers for themselves but are not rich toward God." It seems that being rich toward God is the intended purpose of our lives and its final reward which stores up treasure in heaven that cannot be lost or taken. This comment raises the question of how one becomes rich toward God. That is the real goal of our lives according to these words of Jesus.

> In Joseph F. Girzone's novel, *Joshua,* the main character and Christ figure, Joshua, becomes a popular celebrity at the synagogue and one evening the rabbi invites him to address the congregation.
> "You become what you love, and when you love the things of this world you lower yourselves to the level of those things. It is unworthy of you to crave them and set value on them as if they bestow upon you a dignity. They have value only as reminders of the world where God lives. To love them in themselves is to drink from the polluted well Jeremiah talked about." [10]

An important part of the issue with the accumulation of wealth is that we can come to love these material goods and what they may

10 Joseph F. Girzone, *Joshua: A Parable for Today,* (Toronto: An M & S Paperback from McClelland & Stewart Inc., 1983, 1987), p. 197.

offer or what we believe they offer, but the serious danger is that your love shifts to these created goods and away from the true God and owner of all that is. When we love and hold in first place those entities which are not the true God that is idolatry. It can be tempting sometimes to believe in and trust the things that we can see rather than the God whom we cannot see. Yet these things that we can see do not give us an abundant life, nor can they offer us life beyond this life. The goods of this world do not offer us forgiveness of our sins, nor a life of experiencing the love and presence of God within and around us.

In his comment, Jesus told those who were listening where the true treasure was, namely in being rich toward God. The question arises about *how* we become rich toward God, who is referred to as the "pearl of great price" (Matthew 13:46) and "a treasure hidden in a field" (Matthew13:44)? If I were to ask that in this gathering there would be differing answers this question. What would you say to such a question?

It might be helpful to look around us and see who among us is rich toward God? What does that look like and what does it act like?

> H.M. Stanley was the newspaper reporter who went looking for Dr. David Livingstone in Africa after he had been out of contact with the world beyond Africa for quite some time. When Stanley finally did find the missionary in Africa he said of him, "If I had been with him for much longer, I would have been compelled to become a Christian and he never spoke a word of it to me."[11]

Dr. Livingstone made such an impact upon the world through his dual professions as both a missionary and a medical doctor. He was willing to leave the comfort and familiarity of life in Scotland to go to the yet unknown territory of Africa and to serve there. He not only preached the gospel and served as a doctor to those whom he encountered but he also became famous for his taking a stand against the slave trade.

A major achievement and legacy of David Livingstone was his account of the Myangwe massacre which caused a public outcry in Britian and forced the government to act in 1873. The sultan of Zanzibar signed a treaty which abolished the East Africa slave trade.[12]

---

11 *Emphasis: A Preaching Journal for the Parish Pastor*, vol.24, No.1, May-June 1994, (Lima, OH: CSS Publ.Co., Inc.) p.33

12 http://www.davidlivingstone-birthplace.org/legacy

Here is an expression of a Christian who was willing to serve where he felt there was great need, even though it involved a lot of him. He not only gave what he had to offer in terms of skills and faith, but he also advocated for the plight of those who were being enslaved in Africa. Through his speaking up an important and needed change happened for those who being taken in slavery.

A life rich toward God has God at the center of it, because of this primary focus in the life of such believers it is manifest in the choices they make, the things they do and the love expressed which reflects the love of the divine. To have an existence that is rich toward the divine involves having invested in cultivating what has been given initially through the Holy Spirit, grace and the working of the word. Love of God is like other kinds of love in that if it is to grow strong it needs to be fed and fostered.

In this text, the issue is indirectly lifted up about where are we investing ourselves, where are we spending our hours, attentions, our passions, and efforts? It is a matter of priorities. What is really most important in our perspective and in our living experience?

There was a man who truly loved his family and so in an effort to provide well for them he got a well-paying job. It had a lot of responsibilities with it that took him away from home, required long hours of work and even his sleep and times off were disturbed by calls from work. His wife tried to get him to slow down, and to spend more time with her and the family, but to no avail.

Eventually his marriage failed and he was heartbroken. That was not what he had expected to happen. Where do we spend our time, our attention, our resources in have many impacts upon our daily life and even our future? Does our life serve our highest priorities?

A life rich toward God involves spending time, attention, our love, and efforts to growing a deeper relationship with God. Yes, we are rescued from judgment and death by the work of grace that gives us faith which saves us for life. What does this salvation by the efforts of Christ mean for our everyday living? It can be like getting married. Yes, we have a spouse, but now what? How will that intimate and important relationship develop or not depends on the way we relate to our spouse and the kind of effort and attention that we are prepared to invest into that relationship. How does the love we carry find expression? What kind of decisions do we make based on the importance of that vital relationship?

There are some decisions that we can make which help deepen our relationship with God. Regularly attending worship services is important. It is where we can hear the word, receive the sacraments, and share the faith with others in community. In addition to that we can attend a Bible study and read the scriptures at home. Then there is the importance of prayer as a means of continuing personal contact and communication with God. This is an important arena where the desires of our hearts can be expressed. If the Spirit leads us to a deepening desire for a better relationship with the Lord of love, then we can act on that prompting which leads into perspectives or practices that will draw us closer to the divine.

If we are attuned to the word of God, we learn about the ways that God would have our love find expression. We are challenged to love God firstly and to love neighbor as ourselves. If we love God then we will want to do as we are instructed. In John 15:12-14 Jesus said, "This is my commandment that you love one another as I have loved you. No one has greater love than this, to lay down one's life for one's friends. You are my friends if you do what I commanded you. I do not call you servants any longer, because the servant does not know what the master is doing, but I have called you friends because I have made known to you everything that I have heard from my Father."

To grow rich with God involves being a good friend of Jesus. The more we appreciate all that he has done for us as our friend the more we trust him, and love him too. Then our love of Christ finds expression in love shown to our neighbors. The more we embody the care of Christ demonstrating it by being a good friend to others around us the more we show ourselves the true friend of Jesus. Then through connection with him to our heavenly parent. The more we love, the more we learn about love and can develop and deepen our capacity to really love not just neighbor but God's own self.

If we desire the better way that leads to a life and relationship of love that will last forever, then it is vital that we live a life rich toward God and the relationships of love that are given us as friends of Christ. When God is our true treasure then we will have gained the better way than relying on the riches of this material world. In the love of God and for God are riches that will bring us the peace, the security, the blessings, and the meaning that we seek in our hearts and minds. In devoting ourselves to being rich toward the divine we will find ourselves made rich in ways that will fill and satisfy our hearts. These great riches from God grant us hope for a life that will not end with the One who has loved us enough to die that we may have life through spending himself entirely for us who are his friends now and always because he has treasured us so much.

Amen.

Proper 14 (19)
Luke 12:32-40

Pleased To Give The Kingdom

H.P. Lovecraft said of fear, "The oldest and strongest emotion of 'humanity' is fear, and the oldest and strongest kind of fear is fear of the unknown."[13]

Fear is a difficult emotion that can deeply disturb us and our lives. We are not at peace when filled with fear. Rather we are on edge, agitated, anxious, apprehensive maybe even paranoid waiting for the next feared event to occur.

To all that we are admonished in Luke 12:32, "Do not be afraid little flock, for it is the Father's good pleasure to give you he kingdom." Implied is that the gaining of the kingdom is an antidote to fear. In the world at present, there is much need for this antidote because there is so much fear about so many situations and dangers associated with them. Fear is everywhere and troubling people in so many ways. Fear can be such a strong feeling which can inhibit us or disturb us so that we are unable to move ahead because of what we dread. The anxiety of what we do not yet know can make us retreat to what we do know where we feel more secure. How many good intentions have not been pursued or fulfilled because of uneasiness of the unknown? Fear can also leave us feeling helpless to deal with this big scary thing which we feel is unmanageable. That kind of fear can immobilize us as well. Furthermore, fear is stressful which takes its toll on the body, mind and spirit.

There are situations which certainly can create fear. There were a rash of violent encounters on the transit trains in the city of Edmonton. Riders were also accosted at transit stations which led to a reduction in ridership until security guards were hired to patrol some of the most violence prone areas. There was a practical impact because of the fear felt by those riding the transit system.

The story is told of a burglar who entered the house of a poor country pastor long after midnight. As he was fumbling

13 https://www.brainyquote.com/authors/h-p-lovecraft-quotes

through some drawers, the minister entered the room. The burglar pointed his gun at the parson and said: "Don't move or you're a dead man. I'm hunting for your money."

"Well, you've got faith, I must say!" the minister responded. "How about letting me hunt with you."[14]

So many people are afraid of what is happening in the world around them. Then there are those who have experienced harmful and distressing events that have left them traumatized. It doesn't take much to trigger the feelings of panic and worry about what might happen in the present. All kinds of catastrophes have been happening around the world. Tornadoes, massive floods, major forest fires, and droughts. We hear a lot about the dangers of global warming and wonder what will happen in the future because of it, what of those most harmed by it and will we be directly affected by it. What about all the pollutants in the world, or the plastic waste that seems to be everywhere even entering our bodies because of the microscopic size of particles of it in the water and soil.

What is happening in the country and in relation to the actions of governments that impact on the lives of citizens? What about the high rate of drug use and the loss of life with it? Then there are the continuing issues around violence in homes, on the streets, on schools, and in the world. All these dynamics can cause us to feel unsafe and unsure about what is going to happen. As H.P. Lovecraft said, "The oldest and strongest emotion of 'humanity' is fear, and the oldest and strongest kind of fear is fear of the unknown."[15] There is lots that is unknown in our world at this point in history.

In the face of all that we are encouraged to fear not because it is the pleasure of the Father to give us the kingdom. Instead of fear the heavenly parent is feeling pleasure in giving us the treasure of the kingdom even in the midst of the world so troubled by fears.

In a way it may be surprising to us that it in the giving of the kingdom, the feeling stirred within God is one of pleasure. Emotion is stirred in the heart of the divine to grant us the gift of God's reign and what that means to us and this world. That pleasure is connected to the care of the heavenly parent for us. I remember a young a mother would make dresses for her two daughters. It gave her a sense of satisfaction as well as pleasure to make those dresses and to see the

14 *Emphasis, A Journal for the Minister;* vol.13, No. 3, August 1, 1983, p. 11.

15 https://www.brainyquote.com/authors/h-p-lovecraft-quotes

daughters wearing them. Later in life when she no longer needed to make clothes for her girls, she made simple dresses as well as shirts and shorts for children who had none or only a few garments in other countries. Again, it gave her pleasure to feel that she was contributing to the needs of children. In the same way, God as a parent wants to see us cared for, not just physically but emotionally and spiritually as well, as he does not want to see our lives hampered and hemmed in by fears.

God is taking action to provide for us even in the face of what we fear. In trust and certainty about the good will of our heavenly parent toward us, we are not to be afraid we are being given the kingdom. One might wonder how gaining the kingdom can alleviate our fears. It may help to know more about what is meant by the kingdom of God as mentioned in the text.

The book of Isaiah holds forth the vision of a new and better world that God will usher in at some point through the work of an agent mandated by the almighty. Isaiah 4:2-4 states that Zion will become the highest of all mountains. Then the people of the nations shall come to it in order to learn what God will teach there so that they might walk in those ways. Furthermore, the one in Jerusalem will settle differences between peoples and nations so that there will be peace. Because of the stable political setting, "They shall beat their swords into plowshares, and their spears into pruning hooks. Nation shall not lift up the sword against nation, neither shall they learn war anymore."

So much apprehension is caused by war and the threat of war in our world. There was an item on the news feed for May 21, 2024, about young people in Myanmar rising up against the military junta there. They were ill-equipped and yet they gathered to gain some basic military training in order to struggle against the military that has taken control of their country. Won't it be wonderful when such training and such conflict costing many lives as well as causing serious injuries, will be no more? The kingdom of God will be a realm of peace instead of fear.

Isaiah 11: 6-9 takes this dominion of peace even further even to the animal species of the earth, then predation shall cease, so even the animals will not have to experience fear of being stalked and killed. "The wolf will lie down with the lamb, the leopard shall lie down with the kid, the calf, the lion and the fatling together and a little child shall lead them. The cow and the bear shall graze, and their young shall lie down together; and the lion shall eat straw like the ox. The nursing child shall play over the hole of the asp, and the weaned child shall put the hand on the adder's den. They shall not hurt nor destroy on all my holy mountain." This world will function so differently than the present one. The peace that the day of the Lord is expected to usher in will be governed in harmony not only for human societies, but even the creation will participate in this new order without the interference of fear and the threat of harm and death.

Isaiah 35:1-7 presents a vision of water being provided to dry areas so that they become fruitful. Impediments at that time will be healed. Those who are weak will be strengthened. The blind, deaf, lame and mute will regain their capacities. The time when things will be as God desires will bring restoration to those who have suffered disabilities and frailties. All will be healthy and well which is what the divine wants for us even now.

Daniel 7:13 provides a vision of the coming of the human being who would usher in this new realm and order for creation. He will arrive in the clouds, and to this one will be given dominion, and glory and the kingship so that, "all nations and peoples of all languages will serve him. His dominion is an everlasting dominion, that shall not pass away, and his kingship is one that shall never be destroyed."

What Jesus was saying in the comment, "Have no fear little flock, for it is your Father's good pleasure to give you the kingdom" is the inference that God desires for the little flock to have all these wonderful benefits promised to those who inhabit the kingdom of God. The pleasure of the heavenly parent to grant us through grace, the gifts of peace, health, and hope for what is yet to come. Even if we do not yet have these blessings of full health and well-being at the moment, the hope is that one day the Messiah will return and complete the work begun already in this world. In the meanwhile, he is working at setting us free and granting us aid and mercy.

A person at church following the worship service said in conversation that he believed that healing was happening week by week through the work of the divine, present and working in the midst of the church service and community.

In Jesus, the coming of this reign is already revealed in the exorcisms he performs where he overcomes the powers of darkness and opposition to God. The casting out of evil shows that in him the end times are already begun. Jesus demonstrates power and authority even over the forces opposed to the divine and the agenda of God. The importance of his works is pointed out in his reply to those whom John the Baptist sent to inquire if Jesus really was the one. Jesus sends the answer to this question, "Go and tell John what you have seen and heard: the blind receive their sight, the lame walk, lepers are cleansed, the deaf hear, the dead are raised up, the poor have good news preached to them" (Luke 7:12, Matthew 11:4-5). While Jesus was not clearly identified as the Messiah, yet he lifted up to John his power to perform miracles and healings, which pointed to the fulfillment of the prophetic texts about life in the kingdom to God. (Isaiah 29:18-19; 35:5-6; 61:1)

In Jesus' person and ministry the work and evidence of the kingdom are manifest, even in a germinal form although it is not entirely in force yet amid the workings of this world. The disciples as the initial little flock begin to receive the kingdom and its benefits as they follow Jesus in faith. They will also witness to the working of the kingdom in the person of Christ.

The Interpreters' Dictionary of the Bible, makes this observation about the kingdom given as a gift of grace, in the present.

> "So, to receive it means humbly and loyally to submit to God's rule by obedience to the commandments of Jesus. This aspect of Jesus' teaching corresponds to the rabbinic idea of "taking upon oneself the yoke of the kingdom of God..." (Matthew 11:29-30). Those who receive the kingdom in this way institute the present community of the kingdom of God and to them is promised entrance, in the future into the consummated kingdom."[16]

Jesus told the little flock that they would receive the kingdom, and that was quite a statement. How are we the little flock belonging to the divine in our time and place respond to this gift? How does God want to work to bring the power of the kingdom to bear where we are? As we and those who join us, follow Jesus and witness to his work may we see for ourselves the reign of God breaking into this world. In the face of what frightens us God is still at work and in faith we can move forward into the unknown and the apprehension it brings us believing

16 *Interpreter's Dictionary of the Bible, Illustrated Encyclopedia.* Vol. 3, K-Q (Nashville: Abingdon, 1962) p. 24.

that God is there ahead of us and working to bring us good because of the divine pleasure in doing just that for us.

Even today as the followers of Jesus we read of his miracles, and at times see them enacted. May we continue to see the realm of the divine breaking into this world and not lose hope. Even today the word of Christ speaks and calls us to follow his teaching and what he modeled for us. As we seek to grow closer to him, and deeper in our faith we too can experience the wonderful peace that is part of that kingdom. As the church continues with healing ministry it is testimony to the good pleasure of the heavenly parent who wants us to be whole and well. Relying on the pleasure of the divine to bring us the help, the harmony and the hope we need we continue to pray and to work toward being an agent of the kingdom here and now as well as rejoicing in the work and will of God.

In order to move out into the world as those who are carrying the kingdom in and among us, it is important that we have faith that God is at work for, in, and through us too, instead of just being scared of the unknown. In hope of the in-breaking of the divine through Jesus and his work we can have a sense of his capacity at work in and among us. That can help move us past the fear and anxiety that would stop us or hamper us in our lives and in the movement to serve as witnesses. The kingdom is with us and the good that God desires for us and the world goes with us even as Christ goes with us.

As Jesus encountered a need or ailment, he did not turn away, but he provided what would restore health and wholeness. Even when he was opposed by the Pharisees who would have silenced and dismissed him, he was not afraid and continued to do what he had come to accomplish in the lives of those whose paths he crossed. In the face of threat and opposition he continued to do the work of the kingdom, healing, teaching and challenging the forces that would thwart his mission and stop him.

Jesus continued forward even in the face of the terrible threat that lay in his future at Jerusalem, which was not unknown to him. He could have turned away in fear, but instead he moved ahead into those events that lay ahead of him. Even the most dreaded fear of death did not stop him from moving forward to do what he needed to do in order to save us by the power of his forgiveness and sacrifice. Only then could the gospel be carried out into the world so that others could believe, have faith in him and experience the beginning of the kingdom in their lives. Jesus' faithful witnesses carried out the message of this one who ushers in the kingdom of God and who calls people from all over the world to come and belong, through faith. Belonging to the little flock and being a source of pleasure to the heavenly parent as the beginning of the kingdom is given to them as well.

Even though the disciples and apostles had to face all kinds of fearful experiences they did so from within the context of the kingdom. As they set out into the unknown and no doubt, they too felt fear like most of us do in those circumstances. Nevertheless, they went because they knew that the Christ and the power of his love was with them. In faith and trust they continued to do what they had been mandated to do, speaking of Jesus and continuing his work. In the face of fears, they did do what he had asked them to do for the sake of the kingdom. Then because of their love of the leader who loved them and us enough to suffer and die for them and for all of our sakes, they moved out as agents of the beginning of the kingdom. They carried its hope and power with them. In some ways the world was changed through the message and the work of the kingdom of God in the nations where the little flock of Jesus went to carry his work and message out into all the world.

We do not need to face our fears alone. Jesus is with us, and we too belong to the little flock. There is support in being a part of that little flock who shared the pleasure of the heavenly parent who has made us a part of the kingdom. Jesus rose from the dead having faced what we most fear, in order to be with us. When he is present the power of the heavenly kingdom is already at work to bring freedom from sin, the power of his teaching, and the work he does as he seeks to bring us healing of all kinds of things that harm us or cause us fear. Jesus and the heavenly parents are working that we might experience the shalom or the peace that is so much a part of the kingdom and begin to live in the wholeness desired for us.

Amen.

Proper 15 (20)
Luke 12:49-56

Fire

Jesus said that he came to bring fire to the earth. In Greek mythology Prometheus also brought fire to human beings because he felt sorry for them. Prometheus stole fire from the altars of the gods and brought it to humans. Fire is a powerful entity. Because of fire humanity could inhabit and survive in colder parts of the world than would be possible otherwise. Heat is also necessary for the cooking of food, all over the world. Apparently human beings are designed to eat cooked food and are the only species that does. Most animals who eat forage such as grass have longer and more complicated digestive tracts than people do in order to break down the starches and cellulose found in forage. Whereas by cooking, human beings are able to eat starchy foods processed with the use of heat that begins the digestive process. This use of fire to cook food has enabled human beings to move away from such a heavy reliance on meat, fish, and fruit to having starchy foods as a major food source to sustain life. Fire is a necessary part of human life. When Jesus brought fire, he was not bringing us a strange and foreign entity but using an image of something that is common and important in the human experience.

While fire has its needed and helpful attributes it also has the capacity to destroy and to bring radical change. There have been so many forest fires raging in various parts of the world over the past few years. Yet what is left behind is much the same. There are blackened tree trunks, burned out vehicles, the rubble of ash, and the ruin of the buildings that were there before. This potential to do such harm and even to destroy certainly causes fear and panic when confronted by a raging fire.

Generally, we look for stability and resist the demolition brought by fire. Many of us are opposed to change, especially the radical and devastating alteration fire would bring. Yet change is woven into the nature of life in this world because of our mortality. We change, decay, and disappear from the framework of this world, even as do things around us. Not far from home was an old, dilapidated building. The roof was badly swayed and the whole building was tilting to one side. We wondered how long it would be until it would cave in on itself and fall to the ground. Not long ago when we drove by it, and we saw a pile of rubble where the building once stood. One wonders if the owner of it will set a match to it one of these days. In such circumstances fire can clear away what is no longer of use.

As the material world changes there is need to let go of some things, or even to destroy them in order that something new and useable can grow up or be built. Have you noticed that when old grass and weeds are burned the new growth that comes up afterward is often so green and lush? The old plant materials in the decaying form tie up the minerals. When there is a fire, these minerals are released and since they are in their elemental form they are easier for new plant life to absorb and use for growth.

Fire by its nature destroys but also can make way for the new. In the text Jesus said that he wished that the fire he brought was already kindled. It is something that he foresaw as happening in the future and seemed eager to see that flame start. In the next sentence he said that he had a baptism with which to be baptized, and that he was under stress in anticipation for that to happen. It would seem the fire he brought has to do with the baptism of which he speaks.

Jesus had already been baptized by John in the River Jordan — now he awaited another baptism. Are there parallels between these two baptisms for him? In his life baptism marked a radical change in the direction of his life and purpose. As Jesus rose from the water of the Jordan and went out into the wilderness then began his public ministry. His life was filled with activity travelling to various places to teach, to heal, and to set free those who were oppressed and give hope to the poor.

The second baptism of which Jesus spoke also marked a radical change in the course of his life and ministry. In his suffering and death, he moved from being teacher, healer, and mentor for his disciples to the very different role as the lamb of God. In order to inaugurate this shift, he faced great suffering and a horrible death on the cross.

Then instead of rising from the water of the Jordan, he rose to new life from the tomb where his body had been placed. In the resurrection he began a radically new kind of life that he shared with the world and changed the course of history. Jesus rose to new life in order to serve as the savior and redeemer of all who are gathered to him by grace and the working of the Holy Spirit. He knew that this second baptism would be painful unlike his first baptism, and so it is understandable that he was under stress until it was completed. Yet our lives and futures are radically changed by the fire of his second baptism, even as we are baptized for the first time into his baptism of suffering and death, to begin a life as his disciple.

Through Christ's anguish at the hands of his enemies, and then dying such a painful and humiliating death, it could certainly be classified as a fire because the intention of these actions was to destroy him finally and completely. Yet what came out of those actions would be another kind of a fire that would burn down old ways or perspectives and institute a radically different kind of a covenant than had been in place up to that point. Rather than having to offer sacrifices to cover one's sins, now a person could find forgiveness through the person of Christ. Jesus' second baptism opened the way to eternal life for those who believe and have faith in him who died for their sakes. Jesus came to call us from the old ways into a new life in him though the working of the Holy Spirit, and the power of the word.

Sometimes in listening to or reading articles or books about Celtic culture and society with the coming of Christianity there is a lament that the old ways, and the old spirituality was fading away. Although some of the threads of that perspective did find their way into the form of Christianity as it took root in those lands. There was certainly a sense of the old giving way and the new life and faith in Christ coming like a fire to bring a radical change in belief and practice.

Sometimes the radical change comes to individuals as well such as happened to C.S. Lewis who while raised in the church had turned from it. He described his shift from atheism that he had embraced, to Christ.

> You must picture me alone in that room in Magdalen [College, Oxford], night after night, feeling, whenever my mind lifted even for a second from my work, the steady, unrelenting approach of him whom I so earnestly desired not to meet. That which I greatly feared had at last come upon me. In the Trinity Term of 1929 I gave in, and admitted that God was God, and knelt and prayed: perhaps, that night, the most dejected and reluctant convert in all England.

After his conversion to theism in 1929, Lewis converted

to Christianity in 1931, following a long discussion during a late-night walk along Addison's Walk with close friends Tolkien and Hugo Dyson. He records making a specific commitment to Christian belief while on his way to the zoo with his brother. He became a committed member of the Church of England.[17]

When the fire of Christ's spirit and grace are at work in human hearts and minds there is a letting go of old and even wrong ways of thinking and believing. Then the radical change brought by accepting the reality of Christ and the light of the great love he brings which seeks us and draws us into relationship with him. As we live with him as disciples, he is at work to overcome and help us leave behind old, unhelpful or unloving attitudes, beliefs, and actions. He came to turn us from old and worldly ways and thinking. By the Spirit we grow in understanding and experience of his great love and mercy to us. Thus, cultivating devotion that loves him in return and seeks to live in harmony with the divine being guided by the words and directions given by God.

Jesus never made following him an easy path. He asks for our unqualified devotion, even if it means putting parents, children, and our own lives second and him first. It is small wonder he had so many fascinated followers but only twelve dedicated disciples.

In regard to the cost of following Christ, there is an ancient legend that comes from Ireland when St. Patrick was baptizing newly converted Christians in the River Boyne. Patrick waded out waist-deep and turned, calling the new Christians to follow him one by one. The first, a brave and scared chief from the mountains of Connemara, stepped out into the water until he was standing next to Patrick. The bishop, who had been holding a staff aloft, brought it down to stick in the river bottom, while with both hands he lowered the chief beneath the water and baptized him in the name of the Father, the Son, and the Holy Spirit.

But the chief was seen to limp as he made his way back to the shore. Later someone told St. Patrick that when he had brought down his staff to rest on the riverbed, it had glanced off and broken the foot of the chief. Patrick went to

17   https://en.wikipedia.org/wiki/C._S._Lewis

him at once: "Why didn't you cry out? Why didn't you stop me when I struck your foot?" And the chief looked at him with astonishment and said, "I remembered about the nails you told us about in the cross," he said, "And I thought it must be part of the baptism."

Sometimes blows and nails wounds are only a small part of the cost of what comes when ... we follow Jesus Christ.[18]

Jesus is giving his disciples warning. Not only will he have to go through a baptism of fire that involves such suffering, and those who follow him will also have troubles, distress and their own forms of fire to deal with because of their following of him.

There is a word of caution that he does not come to bring peace but division. That is a tough word for us, we do not want to have division and conflict, especially not in our families and yet our allegiance to Jesus may bring such tension and brokenness into the family circle.

Sometimes, for the sake of peace, families have turned away from actively participating in the worship and community of faith. A couple may come from families who belonged to different denominations, and instead of favoring one over the other they have chosen to withdraw from participation. The problem is that they then are not feeding their faith by regular worship attendance, and their children and grandchildren also miss out on hearing the gospel message and being disciples of Jesus. In an effort to keep the peace the family misses out on what would grant and cultivate faith. They also may not receive the many blessings that the Christian faith brings even through the fire of suffering that accompanies it.

Because of the call of Christ to a deep loyalty over other relationships, many in the western world have turned away from the faith, preferring different priorities which seem easier and more desirable. There is an issue of conflict that arises also for those who come into the Christian faith from other faiths. When people are drawn into a new life in Christ that may put them at odds with their families. It may cause friction between them and other family members who would feel that they are being disloyal to leave their traditional religious background to join with Jesus and the community around him. In some contexts that converts' very life may be in danger, along with their family's welfare.

---

18 *Emphasis, A Journal for the Minister,* August 1, 1983, vol.13, No.3, p.20

Masih was an active Islamic student and argued with Christian students. He couldn't understand their opinions. Eventually they offered to help him learn more about Jesus. He had many questions about Jesus which they answered.

But Masih was not satisfied. He went to some Muslim clerics who were his friends. They said, "Christians told you this. Don't be deceived by them." Masih felt they were avoiding his questions and pressed them for specific answers. In the end they gave the same answers that the Christians did.

Still, Masih needed more proof. He eventually went to another religious leader who was a friend...he said, "What Christians told you is true. But if you tell others, people will kill you."

When Masih heard this, he went to a Christian pastor. He told him about Jesus as Savior by using both the Koran and the Bible. Masih slowly came to the realization that the Koran did not tell the whole story about Jesus. In his own heart he realized that Jesus was the truth and that sincere believers of truth must follow Jesus.

After that, his family kicked him out. His brother threatened to kill him. His parents claimed that he had been kidnapped by Christians and accused the Christian pastor. Masih testified in court and cleared the pastor of the charges. Then he hid with Christians in another city and went to a seminary.

His brother in Jordan invited him to visit and told him not to tell the Jordanians that he was a Christian. Then when he heard the Masih had become a pastor he and his family did not want to see him again. So indeed, he had lost his family because of his choice to become a disciple of Jesus

He says, "I am now an ordained pastor, and I was married two months ago. I am happy in Jesus. Although I have lost my physical family, I have a spiritual family. Now I help Christian brothers and sisters to understand Muslims and lead them to Christ."[19]

The truth about the warning of the cost of discipleship is the lived experience of many around the world. During the twentieth century the highest number of Christians were killed for their faith. Yet in

19 DC Talk and the Voice of the Martyrs, *Jesus Freaks; Stories of Those who Stood for Jesus The Ultimate Jesus Freaks*, (Tulsa, Oklahoma: Albury Publ.,1999), pp.52-53

the west with our policies of religious tolerance this warning may not have the same impact as for those who are shunned and rejected or threatened for their loyalty to Jesus in other parts of the world.

It is a tough reality to live in a state where father will be against son, and son against father, mother against daughter, and daughter against mother, mother-in-law against daughter-in-law and daughter-in-law against mother-in-law. Conflict in family relations is such a difficult thing. That deep sense of belonging and of a shared history can be lost in conflict over loyalty to Jesus. Jesus knows that this will happen to some. He understands how difficult this kind of fracture can be to live with and yet he still calls people to come and gain new life in him even in the face of such a tearing apart of family connections.

The issue arises about where our deepest loyalties lie, even in such a personal level as in regard to our familial relationships. One can see how torn and distressed someone caught in the situation of losing their familial connections can be. It is not small thing to follow Christ sometimes. So then how much does Jesus, through who he is and what he had done for us, mean to us? Masih was clear that Jesus was of vital importance even when it cost him family connections and acceptance, he continued on in loyalty to Jesus.

In a way, what Masih went through was another form of a baptism of fire. Again and again his family pressured him to return to their religion and traditions. Yet Masih was adamant in his devotion to Christ and would not be swayed or pressured to stray from his faith in Jesus.

What about us when we run into opposition to our faith and devotion to Jesus? Are we firmly enough planted in connection to him that we can withstand the time of challenge, even from those closest and most important to us? It is in such "fires" that we are tested and shown to be loyal and devoted disciples or are we those who fall away under pressure, rejection and loss? How much is Jesus and what he has done for us really worth to us?

Amen.

Healed To Stand Tall

Jesus was doing what you are doing this morning. He was at worship on the Sabbath. Not only was he in the synagogue but he was teaching. Being at the front of the synagogue he could see what was going on in that space.

What did he see? A woman coming in who was bent over because she couldn't straighten up. She was likely elderly because most people struggling with being so bent over are older. Jesus' interaction with this woman was very public as he called her to come up to him in front of the whole congregation and declared that she was set free from the ailment. Jesus went from teaching to addressing the physical issues of one who had come into worship. That was followed with his laying his hands on her. Between the spoken word and the touch of Jesus she was finally, after eighteen long years, able to straighten up. Likely she would have had a lot of pain from her back and that would have disappeared as well.

Probably there were other issues that went with having a bent back. I remember a conversation with a chiropractor who spoke about all the functions of the body that were associated with the back. When the back is "out of alignment" all kinds of other problems can arise. Therefore, one wonders what other kinds of ailments and pain went with her back condition. So, when Jesus straightened her back all those other attendant problems, pains, and weaknesses also would have been cleared up. One can only imagine her celebration upon leaving the synagogue that day!

Furthermore, this woman's perspective and experience of the world around her would have been radically altered by her condition of having a bent back. Imagine what her view of the world was before that Sabbath day. Slowly over time as she had bent further and further forward, she got so she had a great view of the floor, the ground and the paths where she went. How much would a person bent over miss because she was not able to physically see it since her eyes would be focused downward?

I remember one faithful soul who joined me for worship at a seniors' facility when I lead services there. He too was very bent over and occasionally would comment on the pain. Yet in the face of that pain, he still made his way to worship. He also would be at coffee time following the service, and gladly participate in the discussion. However, if he wanted to see a speaker, he would tuck his hand under his chin and physically lift his head as much as he could so he could see others around him.

There were so many other things involved in living with a bent back, and would include a curtailment of one's ability to enjoy the world around them and even the expressions on the other faces around them. We talked about this ailment of the man bent over and he so longed to be healed of his infirmity like the woman in the story today. In faith he had earnestly prayed for such a return to having a straight back. Yet he was disappointed that his requests went unanswered, but he looked forward to the time after death when he would be restored to full health and stature.

Those of you who have back pain or have had back pain can certainly appreciate the plight of this woman at the synagogue that morning. You know what back pain is like. It is such a challenge to live day by day in such suffering. Enduring pain for years on end wears on a person not only physically but mentally, spiritually and emotionally as well. It certainly has a big impact on the quality of one's daily life.

Thank goodness that there is surgery these days that can alleviate that misery of many people. We are thankful for the medical profession and the help that they can delivery to some of those who are struggling with back pain. Thankfully for the woman who attended worship that day when Jesus was present, she got the attention and help needed without an incision or even physiotherapy.

Sometimes though, people find themselves living "bent over" even though their back is straight and fine. Who among us carries so much inner pain, disappointment, and trauma that they wind up being turned in on themselves. They are emotionally and mentally "bent over" trying to protect themselves, coping with a hidden inner distress that is immobilizing them. In that state they wind up with a reduced perspective about what is around them, perhaps fearing the unseen threats that lurk and might cause pain or loss. Because of their limited vision they find themselves caught in less than ideal situations but they lack the perspective or even the confidence to move in a better direction. Their lives become small. These ones also need the word and the touch of Jesus to help lift them up. Jesus' presence, care and aid are as much needed by those who are "bent over" within themselves as for the woman who came into the synagogue. Fortunately, Jesus sees them even as she saw the woman with the bend over back as she entered the synagogue while he was teaching.

Jesus did not put off what he knew he could do for this woman. After all she had endured the pain for eighteen long years. Surely, he could have offered her his healing following the service rather than disturb the flow of what was going on in the worship service. But that is not what he chose to do. Rather he called her forward. Right there and then he was going to take action for her and her welfare. In that there was a sense of urgency. He did not want her to endure what the bend over condition had brought into her life for one more minute. Jesus took action immediately, right there and then. It seems to me that Jesus was impatient with this ailment and wanted to see the distress it caused to be ended promptly. It is as if he said, "Not a minute longer."

One gathers from this situation that Jesus did not want us to have to drag along suffering and disabilities but would rather see us healed and set free from these kinds of infirmities. In this he is working against the evil that is contrary to the will of the divine for us. When we find ourselves in a lot of pain it is helpful to know that this is not the intention of the divine that we should suffer, but who wills wholeness for us instead. It is important to be reassured that Jesus, the heavenly parent, and the Spirit do not want to see us caught in pain and conditions that limit our lives and curtail the living of our lives as intended by God.

Jesus standing there in that place of worship told the woman that she was set free from her ailment and layed his hands on her. Immediately she stood up straight and started praising God. Actually, it was a wonderful thing that she was healed in her place of worship while being present in the place designated for the work of the holy. In that place her response was praise. The power of Jesus' word and his touch were sufficient to provide the healing that she had longed for eighteen years. What a wonderful thing for the congregation gathered to worship God, to witness there in their midst on a Sabbath day! That should have aided them to worship and praise God for such deliverance of this member of their community, and they joined in the woman's rejoicing.

But not everybody was celebrating. The leader of the synagogue was not pleased because it seemed to him that Jesus' act was inappropriate for the Sabbath especially in the synagogue. In his mind Jesus' deed constituted "work" and so was not to be done on the Sabbath day. One wonders about who this synagogue leader was.

> Local elders governed the synagogue as a kind of democracy. While all adult members of the community could belong to the synagogue, only adult males aged thirteen or older could be elders.
>
> A local caretaker called the *hazzan* (sometimes called "ruler" in the English Bible) was responsible for maintaining the building and organizing prayer services (Mark 5:22, 35-36, 38; Luke 8:41-49; 13:14). The *hazzan* sometimes taught the synagogue school, especially in smaller villages. He would announce the coming Sabbath with blasts on the *shofar* (ram's horn), and he also cared for the Torah scrolls and other sacred writings, bringing them out at the appropriate times (Luke 4:17-20).
>
> Priests and Levites were welcome to participate in synagogue life, including worship, but they had no special leadership role. However, only priests could offer the blessing of Aaron from the Torah (Num. 6:24-27) at the end of a synagogue service.[20]

Here was a person used to caring for as well as organizing the synagogue worship and getting things done. No doubt he had a strong sense of how things should be done. Obviously, Jesus healing on the Sabbath was out of order, and a breaking of the Sabbath laws. He took offense at Jesus and what he had done. But he didn't confront Jesus face-to-face in a private place. No, he held Jesus' action up to public opinion and judgment. What a hostile way to handle this situation and his sense of offense. He said to the crowd, and the text says that he kept saying to them, "There are six days on which to work ought to be done; come on those days and be cured, and not on the Sabbath day." This man would have said to the woman who had come to worship that day, "come back another day." But that was not what Jesus said to her. One can see where this would be grounds for what the leader of the synagogue turned into a public conflict. Surely Jesus knew what the rules about the Sabbath were and yet he chooses to override them

20 https://www.thattheworldmayknow.com/synagogue-leaders

for the sake of the woman worshipper that day. By doing this he indicates that something more important than the keeping of the rules play into this situation.

Jesus was not stopped by the comments and the efforts of the synagogue leader to stir up the crowd against him. He did not just leave because of all the fuss that was being made of his actions. Rather Jesus took the wisest action and replied to the synagogue leader from within the context of the rules about the keeping of the Sabbath. Jesus was teaching at the synagogue service and wound up teaching the synagogue leader as well, who likely was not eager to hear the challenge of Jesus word to his strong sense of the proper behavior on the Sabbath.

Jesus referred to the allowance on the Sabbath to take animals for water, which was common sense. Why would a person allow their animals to languish in thirst even if it is the day of rest? The thirst does not take a day off but requires action so that animals who are not able to get to the water under their own are taken to it. Food and drink are basic requirements for life and those who have animals need to provide for them every day, especially water.

The other day I saw an SUV stopped on a street. The driver had come around to the back of the vehicle and allowed a large dog out. Then he bought out a good-sized bowl and poured water from a jug into it. The dog was obviously thirsty and set to taking a drink. One has to take care of the basic needs of animals who are dependent upon us.

I remember talking to farmers who had livestock. Even on the Sabbath, especially in the winter, they were up early to start their tractors and take hay to their livestock, or feed to indoor animals, as well as to see that the watering system was working. They did this all before they changed their clothes, got into their vehicles and drove to church. Sometimes, particularly cold days their vehicle never made it to the church parking lot because of challenges with their chores.

Jesus used this common practice of providing for livestock and the allowance for it in the regulations about keeping the Sabbath to make his point against the critique of the synagogue leader. To attend to the thirst of one's animals is common sense as well as being an act of mercy. To not water them would have meant to have left them feeling thirsty and driven by that need. We too have been very thirsty at times and understand how miserable of an experience that can be. Therefore, in attending to watering the livestock keeps life normal and settled for them and is an act of consideration toward these living creatures.

If the rules about keeping the Sabbath allow for doing the chores including providing especially water so as not to leave animals in distress, and in intense need, then how much more, Jesus would reason, to attend to the deep needs and distress of a human being, even on the Sabbath. Jesus would not leave this woman who had waited eighteen long years to get some relief from her ongoing suffering. When she showed up at worship and Jesus saw her there in that state. He understood her suffering and that the time for her deliverance from it was at hand. Jesus in his great mercy would not leave her in that misery any longer. Jesus did not countenance her continued pain and limitations, even as those who own animals do not feel it necessary that their animals continue in distress and thirst until the Sabbath passes. Jesus said, "Woman you are set free from your ailment." Then he touched her and she was able to stand tall, finally. In this healing Jesus first spoke a word of liberation to this suffering woman, and then he touched her. Between the power of his word and his touch she was indeed liberated from what had kept her bent over.

As with the animals needing to be freed so they can get to water as an act of consideration and mercy. Likewise, this woman had been set free from her infirmity and pressing desire for help by Jesus who did have care for her and did exercise compassion through the power of his word and touch to her body. She was released and made well. That was an expression of his healing, not only to heal the structures in the body or soul that need correction and reformation. His healing was also an act of setting free. One wonders what that woman had wanted to do for eighteen long years that she had not been able to do. One wonders if she just enjoyed walking around and seeing what she had been unable to see for all that time. What did she do with her new freedom and mobility, after offering praise to God for what she had received? Her joy was shared by those around who were rejoicing in all the wonderful things that Jesus was doing, this healing included.

Furthermore, isn't the Sabbath a perfect day for healing within the context of worship?

In conversation with churchgoers over the years, some of them have felt that Sunday worship has been a place of healing for them. They return week after week open to receiving release from what binds or confines them and their lives. What bends us and limits us, or like the synagogue leader what needs to be challenged in our perspective so that we can become more merciful and loving?

As you and I intentionally show up to worship, Christ sees us as well. Jesus has compassion on us as he did on the woman. He especially works to free us from the effects of evil upon us, which may weigh us down, or bind us and cause us distress. In worship, and as we read the word at home, Jesus speaks through it to us. As he spoke personally to the woman who had arrived to worship. He assured her that she was set free from her ailment. Then when she understood, he layed his hands on her and she was able to straighten up and be released of that which had caused her suffering for all those years.

When we show up for worship as well, God's word is at work within us as well. We present ourselves in order that the word would address us too, sometimes in surprising ways. As we listen and receive what he would grant us, the power of the Christ is at work in us as well. Sometimes we don't even know what is causing us issues, like the synagogue leader. Then how much we need the word of God to speak to us as well, bringing us to change and growth in understanding and compassion. Christ's word also has the capacity to release us from the evil or offenses that we have committed against another. Through the word we may be able to recognize our own offenses even while we are trying, like the synagogue leader to do the right thing. As we confess and hear the word of forgiveness, we are set free and have opportunity to grow in mercy and love toward others.

Christ is at work within us through his word as he helps us and sets us free, so that we can like the healed woman give thanks for the mercy we have received from him and be glad for his kindness and care for us as well even as she did.

Amen.

Proper 17 (22)
Luke 14:7-14

Watch

Some people will go to the mall or sit on a bench in a park and watch people go by and see what they are doing. Jesus was invited to the home of a leader of the Pharisees where he would be watched by the other guests and Jesus would be watching them as well.

Jesus had been invited for a Sabbath meal at the leader of the Pharisee's home on a particular Saturday. One wonders if there were family members present for that meal as well since families tend to gather for the Sabbath meal. If that was so then obviously guests were also invited to join the family for the meal and be a part of time spent together. It may have been a large group gathered as the Pharisees and lawyers had also been welcomed.

When my husband and I were visiting in Israel we went for supper on the Sabbath with the tour group at the hotel where we were staying. One unusual thing we saw that day was that the elevators were set so that they would stop at all floors going up and down, so no one would have to push any buttons. This is a modern adaption of the commandment to keep the Sabbath holy, and to do no work. In the restaurant there was a large group of various aged persons gathered for the evening meal. Our guide told us that they were most likely an extended family group because it is customary to gather to eat together on the Sabbath. Most likely this would have been a part of the Sabbath tradition that Jesus would have experienced in his family's life as well.

That Sabbath, the leader of the Pharisees invited Jesus to come to his home for the meal. It is interesting that such an invitation would be extended to Jesus since there were those present who would have been uncomfortable with Jesus present. He knew there were those in the group of Pharisees and lawyers who disapproved of him, yet he accepted the dinner invitation. One wonders about the motivations of the leader of the Pharisees in his invitation to Jesus. Surely, he must have known about the criticism of the Pharisees toward Jesus and yet he was still invited to the Sabbath meal. Was the leader intrigued or curious about Jesus, or did he want to involve him in discussion? Jesus was not put off by their attitudes but was willing to engage them and their ways of thinking. It was their interpretation of the law that led them to judge him as breaking the Sabbath because of the healing he did even on that day and other Sabbath days.

Those present watched Jesus closely to see what he would do. They obviously ha expectations about Jesus and anticipated what he might do while present, even acts which were contrary to their way of interpreting the law. He set up a confrontation and the challenge knowing this group will raise with him. Perhaps he was hoping to teach them something and to help alter their way of looking at things. Jesus gave them something to see and react to and healed a man suffering with dropsy. But first he inquired of the lawyers if it was lawful to heal on the Sabbath. They did not reply to his question. It would seem that Jesus was prepared for a discussion but those present do not take him up on his query. Nor did their understanding about what was allowed on the Sabbath stop Jesus from offering help and healing.

Jesus continued with his understanding about healing on the Sabbath. He compared healing on the Sabbath to the act of rescuing an animal which had fallen into a well on the Sabbath day, which was legally allowed, for to leave it there well might endanger the life of the animal. Jesus did heal on the Sabbath and the man disabled by dropsy most likely was very glad he did provide the extra beyond the benefit of the meal supplied that day. Imagine that he could now use the utensils supplied for eating along with doing a whole lot of other important things.

Those gathered who were intently watching Jesus to see what he would do, failed to realize that he was also watching them. He would share his thoughts about what he saw them doing around the table. Those present were looking for the best seats at the table for themselves. So why were they doing that? And why did people do that even today? Perhaps they thought they should take the best for themselves. It is rather like getting tickets for a concert of a popular performer when one knows that the tickets will sell quickly. There are those who immediately go to get the best seats they can. Or some are prepared to be in a line for a long time, sometimes even overnight in order to be sure that they get a ticket and hopefully to get the pick of the seat that they prefer. They endure that discomfort and boredom to buy the ticket for a seat and hopefully a good one in order to get the best experience of being present at that event. Likewise, the Pharisees wanted to have the best seat so that they could be near the important guests, to have a chance to talk with them, ask them questions, and to make a connection with this important person. Part of the attraction of the best seats was that it gave some status and sense of importance. What measures are we prepared to go to get the best seat, the best position for ourselves?

When I lived in Calgary, I attended a course with a human resources staff-person in charge of hiring CEOs for positions in oil companies and other businesses that supported the oil patch. She talked about something her company had encouraged the HR staff to do in an effort to discern something of the attitudes and character of the person they were looking for to fill an important position. This HR person doing the interviewing would take the candidate out for a drive to see how they drove on the city streets. What the HR personnel were looking for was an aggressive driver wanting to quickly get to their destination. To that end, some drivers would weave in and out of traffic as well as accelerate quickly from the lights. Those in leadership in that company wanted employees who were energetic, quick to jump in and get things done, as well as not being afraid to make decisions. They believed the way a person drives reflects a general view of how they would operate in their daily lives too. These persons would also be the type of person to take a good seat without asking permission.

Sometimes that take charge attitude is needed. I saw a brief video of a woman who was riding a bicycle on a city street and there was another person standing on the sidewalk right there as she approached. He saw a vehicle that was going to hit her, so he leaped out and grabbed her taking her up onto the sidewalk and out of harm's way. On the video one could see that she would have been hit by the vehicle coming up behind her. Good thing that the fellow on the sidewalk did not hesitate to take the necessary action which saved her from injury and maybe even death.

But this is rather different than the assertiveness of taking the best seats available. What was motivating this behavior and what motivates us when we do likewise. Sometimes we might just want to talk with the people at that table, and to see what is going on, to be in the midst of the action. At other times we want that seat as a way of signaling our status and connection to the hosts or special guests that are present. Often at wedding banquets the best seats are reserved for the immediate family of both the bride and the groom, or special friends.

Not long ago there was a panel discussion of candidates who were running for the leadership of a provincial political party. A couple of them used the opportunity to promote themselves and to ask for those listening to vote for them, instead of sticking to the questions asked about their platform and priorities if elected.

Yet what Jesus taught is not promoted in society at the present time. There was an item on the radio about getting a job in the tight job market. The commentator made the statement that these days, employers are not so much looking for people to fill the requirements on a posting but are looking for the kind of people who will fit into the company and be able to fulfill the mandate of the position well. It suggested that one needed to "sell" or promote their attributes, character, and interests as well as qualifications in applications for positions. The observation made in the article was that many companies are not even posting job openings, rather they look through what they have on file looking for someone who might be the kind of person with the needed skills to do the job. In other words, one is expected to put oneself forward in an appealing way in order to wind up on the short list of applicants, and hopefully move to the top of the list. Looking to get the best seat in the house, is an accepted part of modern life and employment or other opportunities. As a result, this pursuing the best place is promoted in our culture. Jesus would see the same behavior among some of us as he saw at the Sabbath day table. There is so much competition in the way many organizations and even personal relationships function. Yet there is a danger in this way of behaving.

In light of Jesus' observation of the guests seeking and taking the best places at the table, Jesus gave some prudent advice. Using the analogy of a wedding banquet he made the observation that if one takes a seat that the host would rather give to another, the one sitting in that seat would be asked to take another lower seat. This could easily happen at a wedding banquet when the bride and groom have special guests that they want close to them on this important day in their lives, such as parents, siblings, extended family, or significant friends. If another guest was to take that chair one could see where he or she would be asked to find another place. That would result in the one being asked to move feeling humiliated especially if they had to move with a lot of others watching. To lose face is a difficult emotion and social dynamic that we would rather avoid.

Before the guests even sit down, Jesus observed them maneuvering to find and occupy the best seats. In this he saw a teaching opportunity and used it to instruct those gathered. The teaching he provided felt like something out of the book of Proverbs about how to behave in a public function or at important events so as to save face.

In a mediation course, one of the dynamics that students were encouraged to watch for in the negotiating process was that element of "saving face". It is important and helpful that in seeking resolution to the issues at hand be done in such a way that all parties involved do not experience embarrassment or a loss of face. During the meal at the leader of the Pharisees home, Jesus saw those gathered behaving in a way that could bring them a loss of face. He offered a correction that may spare them such discomfort, and us who hear this teaching as well.

Who wants to be humiliated by some breach of protocol? Some people may even avoid participating in certain events because of concern that they may not fit in or know what the protocols are, so they worry about being embarrassed and feeling awkward. Then on account of all that, they chose to not even show up. I sometimes wonder if that is a dynamic for those who are outside the church. Do they avoid entering and participating because they feel like they do not know the protocols and are afraid of making a fool of themselves? How do we work to overcome that anxiety that prevents them coming and joining us for worship and to partake of that which is provided?

I remember while on vacation one time going to a small local church where we had never been before. Quite a number of people turned in their seats to look at my husband and me. It was an uncomfortable and unnerving feeling, although they were welcoming after the service. Another instance concerning seating is when a visitor attends a worship service and takes the seat of a long-time member. Instead of recognizing that the stranger does not know about seating protocols in that congregation and the member being gracious enough to take a different seat that Sunday, rather she or he asks the visitor to move. I expect that the visitor will feel very unwelcome and embarrassed with the result that she or he will very likely not return to worship there again. The visitor will not "come to the table" in the church in the future.

In a practical way this teaching also connects with the teaching that the first shall be last and the last shall be first. At the great banquet at the end of the age, many of those who have held and taken places of honor in society will find themselves in a lower status seats. Those who have been the last and the least will find their place in a more honored seat. It will be the one who observed the maneuvering of the guests at the leader of the Pharisees' house who will be in charge of the seating arrangements. There will likely be some surprises to the guests present.

In the larger scheme of things, a spirit of humility is important, not just at the table but in our relationships with others. If a person is at peace within themself, then there is less need for the status or recognition, and honor of having a higher place over others. Then one is content to just be at the table and present to engage with whoever else is there. That kind of humility also doesn't need to compete with others, but seeks to engage others, take an interest in them and demonstrate care for them as well.

A spirit of humility does not seek to exalt self at the expense of others but rather to love the neighbor wherever they are in social class. The attitude that Jesus is encouraging is one that makes room at the table for others who may not feel like they belong or are wanted at the table. In his great love there is room for all, he desires that they be a part of our community or congregations and the groups that are part of it. How do we make space for others and help them feel like they are welcome? Making space includes having them physically present, talking with them if they are willing, and to be willing to welcome their input and contributions as well.

It is easy to overlook those who do not have status, and yet Jesus calls us to love our neighbors as ourselves, and that involves having a spirit of humility to meet and engage others who are on the edges.

There is such a crisis of loneliness in society these days, and what are so many people longing for these days? They are looking for a place at the table where they will be welcomed and wanted. As church and the people of God do we seek to create a space for them? Are we willing to move over and invite them to sit with us? Then when they occupy that place do we listen well, inviting them to share and be involved as we are able? Do we take the first step to invite others to come and participate with us, or to come and join us at the table? After all the leader of the Pharisees did invite Jesus even though some of the other Pharisees were uncomfortable with him. Nevertheless, the leader did welcome Jesus to come and enjoy the meal with others associated with this leader, and to be a part of the gathering. And Jesus accepted that invitation, even as he would be present in the invitation we extend to others around us.

As we serve Jesus by serving those around us, so as we welcome others to our "table" and activities we are also welcoming Jesus. I expect that he was quite at home with those who have the lowest and least place at the table and in the community that gathers around it. In his openness to others Jesus accepted the invitation of the leader of the Pharisees, even in a climate of criticism. This host was obviously a person of status and Jesus was willing to accept his invitation, showing up at the house and the table. Jesus also would be comfortable with the person with the least prestige, even those who have no place at the table. Jesus in his gracious and open spirit was willing to come to all who would welcome him, at the same time he welcomes all who seek to eat at his table, be with him and converse with him. Jesus extended an invitation, even to those who feel that they have no place at his table. Jesus welcomed them to come and see, and he welcomed us too regardless of where we sit at the table of this world. Jesus wants us to come and eat with him now and as we grow in faith that we might be with him and ever more joyously to eat at his table now and into all of the future.

Amen.

Proper 18 (23)
Luke 14:23-33

Build To Finish

A while ago there were images on the media about protests in Hong Kong of those who were calling for the greater freedoms that they had enjoyed under democratic rule. A number of the leaders of that crowd were arrested by the Chinese police and taken to jail. In June of 2024, sixteen of them had been sentenced, some had been given life sentences, and others did not receive life sentences but had to spend time in prison. One wonders if this group of young people had understood what would happen to them in organizing a protest if they would have done it if they had. The text for today admonishes us to count the cost.

A large crowd was following Jesus, and small wonder with all the healings, the miracles and the teaching that he was providing. It is easy to get caught up in a crowd sometimes and swept along with it. Or we get involved in a group because of others who are also involved, so then we want to belong too. Jesus warned those who have joined the large crowd around himself that there would be a heavy cost to truly being his disciple and going with him. Because there was a heavy cost and challenge to following him, Jesus wanted to warn those around him, encouraging them to count the cost before making the decision to truly follow him. Did they really want to stay with him, even when it led to separation from family, the giving up of their material goods, and to come into suffering, and death?

In that context Jesus said something that was very difficult to hear and to accept. The text reads, "Whoever comes to me and does not hate father, or mother, wife and children, brothers and sisters, yes, and even life itself, cannot be my disciple." This goes against the grain of our normal outlook and interferes with our loyalty and deep connections we have with our families. Sometimes the deepest hurts we carry are from members of our own family, and although the relationship between us may grow strained we do not want to hate them. Hate is a strong word, associated with strong emotion and it seems out of place here. Why should it be necessary to hate those closest to us?

Furthermore, this comment stands contrary to the command of Jesus to love our neighbors as we love ourselves. Our most intimate neighbors usually are our family members, so why would we be told to hate them? Hate seems to be the wrong word. The underlying point though, is that our primary loyalties need to shift to Christ rather than even our closest relationships, let alone others who are not so intimate in our lives. Are we willing to put Jesus first in our relationships and decision making?

The challenge to those who would be disciples of Jesus is that they become like family with him, even more than their family of origin or present family connections. That call goes so far as to ask if we are willing to give up what we have and to lay our lives down in our loyalty to Jesus? That is the ultimate act of devotion, when we give our entire self to follow Christ even our life itself is invested into our discipleship. We, like the rest of the animal kingdom want to survive and live. The challenge to give up even our own life certainly is that goes against the grain. How many people find great purpose in loving and caring for their family members? Most of us do, and we live to care for them and to share our lives with them in the understanding that we are wanted and needed by those who love us. So, we seek to continue living to support those who love us and are dependent upon us. The willingness to die in our discipleship has huge implications not only for us but for those around us especially those closest to us.

> It is told of Queen Elizabeth that when she was a small girl, she was forbidden to do something which she wanted to do. Like any child she was angry. She said, "I am a princess and I will do what I like." King George the Fifth, her grandfather, was there, "My dear," he said, "you *are* a princess and that is the one reason why, all your life, you will never be able to do as you like."
>
> It is so with the Christian. The cost of following Christ is the abandonment of our own wishes and the complete acceptance of His. But this submission is not the broken submission of a slave to a master, or of a subject to a tyrant; it is the submission of love.[21]

---

21 Wm. Barclay, *And Jesus Said: A Handbook on the Parables of Jesus* (Philadelphia: The Westminster Press, 1970), pp. 206-207.

Our closest relationships are so vital and important to us in this world. This statement to hate our loved ones, surely draws a negative reaction from us. I have had people say that their family is first, and they have no intention of changing that. One can certainly understand their response because we feel the significance of family as well.

As we consider this text we wonder if it isn't overstated. Why was Jesus saying this hard thing, and was it a case of overstating what he wanted to get across in order to get people hearing this to stop and really think about what the cost of being a disciple of Jesus involved? It lifted the point that Jesus was calling for a complete commitment from those who would really become his disciple. The upshot of this hard message is that there are those who would have left Jesus and returned to their families and normal lifestyle, and Jesus let them go. The implication was that he was less concerned about the number of those who associate with him. Instead, he sought those who are ready and willing to fully commit to following him. It is important that such people be aware and willing to take the losses, the hardship, and even the death that might attend those who are fully prepared and willing to be a disciple of Jesus.

There is a similar dynamic here to the story of Gideon found in the book of Judges 6-8. The Midianites were opposing the Hebrews, fighting with them and winning because of their more numerous ranks of soldiers. They not only went to war with the Israelites but also destroyed their crops, and livestock. The Israelites cried to God who sent an angel summoning Gideon to deliver the Israelites, promising him success. In response, Gideon gathered troops to fight, but the word came that there were too many who had come and were willing to join the battle. To reduce the numbers, Gideon allowed all those who were fearful to go home, of the 22,000 that had shown up, the number was reduced to 10,000. Again, the word came that even this number was too many. Consequently, he was told to take the troops to the water, and to separate the ones who lapped the water from those who bent down to carry water with their hand to their mouth. Only the ones who had lapped were kept and the remainder were sent home. The number left was only three hundred. With this small group they would surround the camp of their enemy at night, and at the appointed signal they blew their trumpets and broke the jars holding a light. This wake-up call threw the camp of Midianites into confusion when they either fled or took to fighting and killing their fellow soldiers in the camp.

It seems in this text that Jesus was doing as Gideon, and in warning those present about the cost of following him, he encouraged the majority to return home to their families and daily life. A much smaller group would be left to continue to follow Jesus going with him where he went, even to their own cross. He didn't just want numbers but wanted those who were dedicated to him and to go with him wherever that would take them. What was required was a radical letting go of the usual context and even relationships of life.

While I would argue that hating is not required, since we are called to love our neighbors as ourselves, and certainly that would especially apply to those with whom we are closest. However, there needs to be a supremacy to our relationship with Jesus, who dedicated himself to undergoing torture and death for us because it was necessary for our sakes. He went willingly to the cross, putting us first even over his own life.

As one considers the apostles, they did leave their families, and their livelihoods in order to go with Jesus. They did go where he went, then after his death they left their families and faced into a new and unknown future carrying their witness to Jesus even into distant lands. There, as they proclaimed the gospel almost all of them did meet a violent end. The cost of their discipleship was high. Nevertheless, they were so totally committed to Jesus, honoring him and his word to the extent that they were willing to leave behind all that was familiar and those who were significant to them. Sometimes we have to leave some relationships, paths or options for life behind in order to pursue the way of Christ.

> Pastor and Professor Fred Craddock recalled preaching in a university church...some years ago, when a young woman came up after the service. [He] had preached on Mark 1, the call of the disciples. She came up and said she wanted to talk with [Pastor Craddock] and said, "I'm in med school here, and that sermon clinched what I've been struggling with for some time."
> "What's that?"
> "Dropping out of med school."
> "What do you want to do that for?"
> She said she was going to work in the Rio Grande Valley. She said, "I believe that's what God wants me to do."
> She quit med school, went to the Rio Grande Valley, sleeps

under a piece of tin in the back of a pickup truck, and teaches little children while their parents are out in the field. She dropped out of med school for this, and her folks back in Montana were saying, "What in the world happened?"

And [Pastor Craddock] was saying to her, "Well, now, I was just preaching, I didn't mean to, you know."[22] You never know what people will do once they've counted the cost and followed Jesus.

That med student was prepared to count the cost and follow Jesus.

The decisions we make are based on our priorities and that which we consider to be important. The choices we make have impacts on our living and the lives of others. The question is how central is Christ to those choices and have we considered well our options and their consequences in our efforts to be his faithful disciples?

Jesus used a couple of examples to get his point across. The first was about intentions and plans to build a tower. One has to sit down, think through what is to be built, and get an estimate of what it would cost. In our society, one has to also factor in the extra cost that might be entailed above the expected cost.

Recently we called a contractor to build a new fence and he told us upfront that he factors in a 20% charge above the actual cost of the project just in case there are unexpected expenses. After the estimate would we proceed with this project? Do we have sufficient funds to move forward in such a construction project? A half-finished tower or fence is a waste of money and the purpose for which it was built is not fulfilled by a partially completed structure.

There was a family who decided to build a house to live in as they collected funds rather than taking out a loan. For years they lived in the basement which had been poured and roughly finished before they collected sufficient savings to put up the walls and roof for the upstairs. When the structure was closed in, they lived in that unfinished house for a while longer until they had collected enough money to do the finishing work required. However, when the house was finished, they did not have to deal with a debt or the interest on borrowed money. That was the choice they made and the living conditions that

22 Fred B. Craddock, edited by Mike Graves & Richard F. Ward, *Craddock Stories* (St. Louis, Missouri: Chalice Press, 2001), pp. 52-53.

they were prepared to accept in order to complete the project without carrying debt.

A second example given is that of a king wanting to go to war but first considering whether he had enough soldiers to go up against an opponent with twice as many fighters. The issue here is whether the leader has enough resources and strength in his army to win the battle. To pursue armed conflict without sufficient resources or combatants in order to win is foolish. It would result in the slaughter of many people and defeat that would result in major losses of various kinds for the society. Furthermore, it might mean the loss of the monarch's position as leader of that nation or even his death at the hands of an enemy. There could be a very heavy cost to engage in such a war without counting the cost and having the resources to enter into such a battle.

A case in point was the Russian Czar Nicholas II and his army when they got involved in World War One.

> When World War I began in 1914, Nicholas II temporarily strengthened the monarchy by allying with France and Britain against Austria-Hungary and Germany. However, in mid-1915, he made the disastrous decision to take direct command of the Russian armies.
> Every military failure became associated with him, contributing to the discontent that eventually led to the Russian Revolution.[23]

Here is a case where the leader did not sufficiently count the cost of the war in which he had engaged his army and nation in. Nor did he understand the disastrous implications of taking on the leadership of that military without the skills to do so. That lead to a major turn in the history of that nation. He and his family were killed, the monarchy destroyed, and all the chaos created a climate in which Communism could take hold. That, in turn, has had a major impact upon Russia and other nations of the world since that time.

If the cost is not adequately counted and a wrong decision is made it creates major impacts. The entire course of history a nation, a family, or community can be changed by not being ready to meet and pay the costs of important decisions.

Jesus encouraged those in the crowd that had gathered around him to count the cost of the choice of becoming his disciple. While he himself did count the cost of his own work. That was revealed in his

23   BBC — History — Historic Figures: Nicholas II (1868-1918)

predictions of his own death. He knew what price would be paid for his words and works. Jesus understood that his life was on the line, and willingly faced into that terrible price in order to win forgiveness and salvation for us. Thank goodness for Jesus as the leader who was willing to pay such a price for you and I, even as he invites us to follow his way though it lead us to a similar destination as his own.

What strengths and resources do we possess, or can we gain in order to face into a hard struggle that may be required of us as we seek to faithfully follow Jesus? What shall we do when we feel that we do not feel equipped to take up our cross and follow where Jesus has led the way? We are not required to walk that journey alone. Rather the one who walked the way to Mt. Calvary, in his risen state is with us still. And he has promised the resource of the Holy Spirit to provide what we need so that we can respond to challenges before us.

As we seek to follow Christ in trust and love, the resources that we need to work in community with him are available. We rely not only on our own strength and resources, with open hands and hearts we turn to Christ, the heavenly parent, and the Spirit to equip us to do our part. We are not required to do everything needed but to only to play our part as one of those who have counted the cost. We are willing to move forward in a radical trust and reliance upon the Christ who goes before us. With the Spirit we are outfitted with the various spiritual gifts, and powers to engage in the work and service into which the Christ has invited and challenged us, so do we have the will to be and remain a disciple of Jesus?

Having counted the cost of being a disciple we then take our place following Jesus who gave his all for us. Even as we pay the cost may our lives be strengthened in faith, our devotion deepened, and joy increased, and our love made fuller. As we doggedly follow Jesus who went before us, and yet continued with us, then may we become more fully his disciple so that his love and find even greater expression in the living out of our Christian lives and service. May we look to him and the Holy Spirit to lead us and equip us for the discipleship we have accepted and sought to live out for the love of Christ in the power of the Holy Spirit. In the complete devotion we give ourselves and what we have to the love and service of Christ. May we ever more fully experience his love and commitment to care for us and form us into his disciples through this world and into the next.

Amen.

www.ingramcontent.com/pod-product-compliance
Lightning Source LLC
Chambersburg PA
CBHW021508090426
42739CB00007B/525

* 9 7 8 0 7 8 8 0 3 1 2 5 0 *